ME-NOW (MEOW)

The Adventures of
MICKEY THE MUSHING CAT

As told to and written by

Leon S. Mensch

RELEVANT
PUBLISHERS LLC

SUTTON, AK

Visit our website at www.relevantpublishers.com

Relevant Publishers LLC
P.O. Box 505
Sutton, AK 99674

LCCN: 2019917985

Publisher's Cataloging-In-Publication Data
(Prepared by The Donohue Group, Inc.)

Mensch, Leon S.
    Me-Now; The Adventures of Mickey the Mushing Cat/ Leon S. Mensch.

Names: Mensch, Leon S., author.
Title: Me-now / as told to and written by Leon S. Mensch.
Other Titles: Menow
Description: Sutton, AK : Relevant Publishers, LLC, [2020] | Series: The adventures of Mickey the mushing cat ; [1] | Flesch-Kincaid code: 3.1. | Interest age level: 006-009. | Summary: Mickey, the adopted cat, sneaks out of the house and explores a dog sled loaded on top of the family truck. After falling asleep there, he later wakes up in the Iditarod Sled Dog Race, a world-famous race from Anchorage to Nome. Can Mickey and his team survive the 900+ mile journey in bitter cold with other dog teams on the trail that want to eat him?
Identifiers: ISBN 9780999260593 (softbound) | ISBN 9780999260586 (ebook)
Subjects: LCSH: Cats--Alaska--Juvenile fiction. | Sled dog racing--Alaska--Juvenile fiction. | Iditarod (Race)--Juvenile fiction. | Survival--Juvenile fiction. | CYAC: Cats--Alaska--Fiction. | Sled dog racing--Alaska--Fiction. | Iditarod (Race)--Fiction. | Survival--Fiction. | LCGFT: Action and adventure fiction.
Classification: LCC PZ10.3.M52598 Me 2020 (print) | LCC PZ10.3.M52598 (ebook) | DDC [E]--dc23

Printed in the United States of America

DEDICATION

Dedicated to those, without whom, this book would not have been possible:

To my wife, Beth, who provided encouragement, ideas and editing assistance and has put up with me, not only during the writing process but for thirty-five years and counting.

To my sister, Anne, her husband, Patrick, and their children, Jake and Becky. Without them, not only would there be no book, but there would be no Mickey, who they rescued as a stray. They saved him, brought him into our lives, and in some way, saved us.

Mostly, this book is dedicated to Mickey. His curiosity, adventurous nature and loving soul provided the inspiration for this book.

Contents

1

I Hate Snow

Cold, so cold, the first thing I remember is cold. I woke up as the morning light found its way through the cracks in the walls of the frigid old barn where I found shelter. It's been cold and snowing for two days. I haven't been able to find anything to eat in this old barn.

The gnawing pain in my stomach doesn't go away. No food means less energy to hunt and less energy to keep me warm. The constant snow and bone chilling temperature soaked my fur through to my body. My fur was matted down and dripping icy, partly frozen snow. I couldn't feel the tip of my tail, because it had gotten soaked and had crusted over in ice.

There were three cats in the barn before I arrived. I watched them for several days, too scared to enter the barn with them around. When they finally left, I was able to explore this old building. I looked for something to eat. Slowly and silently, I crept around and investigated the broken-down barn. I sniffed around each pile of wood and intently listened at every pile of straw, hoping for evidence of a mouse.

The only scents I found were of the cats that had been here before me. I also smelled the faint vanishing scents of mice long gone from the barn. The only sounds I heard were the ever so soft tapping of the wet snow falling on the metal roof above and the gentle wind, as it whistles through the cracks in the wooden walls of the broken-down barn. I hadn't found any food, but at least I was out of the weather.

I tucked my head tightly into my belly, covered it with my tail, and tried to go back to sleep. I was too hungry and cold to sleep yet too tired to get up to find food. I lay there trying to stop the shivering and trying to ignore the churning aching in my belly. While I lay there, I thought about my life.

I don't know how I got here or where life began. I don't remember my mother or siblings. I just remember the cold, the numbing chill that was always present now. I remember this dilapidated wooden barn that now provided me some shelter from the relentless snow. I also remember the constant hollow feeling in my stomach and weakness that comes from the lack of food.

I finally drifted off into a deep sleep. When I awoke, the snow had stopped. The sun was shining. I stood up slowly and stretched out my cold, stiff muscles. I needed to find something to eat. It was harder to stay warm without food. I hadn't found food in the barn in two days. I needed to venture out into the deep fresh snow to find something to fill my empty belly. I hate snow!

I stood at the door of the barn. I looked out but couldn't see above the fresh snow piled higher than my head. The sun was shining. I hoped the day would warm up. I took that first leap, hoping the snow would hold me. It was too soft and fluffy. I sank up to my neck. I hate snow!

Only my head was spared. I was encased in a blanket of damp bone-numbing snow. All I could see was snow and nothing but snow. I was already cold and now wet, but I kept bounding over the snow for as long as I could without stopping. With each leap, I felt the warm soothing rays of the sun for an instant. Then immediately, the frozen shroud covering the ground surrounded me again.

Eventually, I found a tree to rest under. There was less snow under the tree. I paused under it, trying to warm myself in the sun. I could not rest long. I needed to find food. The day was warming up. The sun felt good on my snow-covered achy body. As I warmed up, the snow slowly started to melt and drip off my soggy matted fur. I gnawed and picked at the ice balls accumulated between my toes. As the sun grew high in the cloudless sky, I slowly dried out and warmed up a little.

I left the shelter of the tree not knowing where I was heading. All I knew was I had to find food. I bounded through the snow for hours until I finally heard a faint sound under the snow. Could it be a mouse?

I stopped and sat in the slowly melting snow silently listening. My ears perked up as the sound pierced them once more. It was a mouse! I tried to pinpoint its location knowing I only had one chance. If I missed, it would be gone.

It was probably only a few minutes, but it felt like hours as I sat silently listening. Then slowly, ever so slowly, I stood up and readied myself. My hind legs were tense and ready to spring. My front paws were light and agile with claws ready to clutch my prey. My ears perked up, twitching left and right to try and pinpoint the sound. My eyes fixated on the point in the snow were the sound was coming from.

I could not see it but located it by the noise it made deep in the snow. Finally, I let loose the springs in my legs. I sprang high above the snow, turning my head down, and landed face first in the snow. I landed right on top of the mouse.

My teeth found the soft fur, dug in, and held on tight. I wrestled my way back to the surface of the snow with my catch. I looked around to make sure no other cats were waiting to steal my breakfast. All clear. Finally, something to fill my belly.

2

I Hate Rain

Luckily for me, the snow didn't last long. I had a few more days of trying to find food in the snow. Then the rain came. The deluge lasted for two straight days. With all the rain, the ground turned from a frozen white blanket of snow to a slippery, pool of wet mush.

My fur and feet were soaked and muddy with no way to dry out. The constant cloudy sky and lack of sun made the daytime just as cold as the night. I wish I had stayed in that old barn. I found a little shelter under some bushes, but I was still cold and wet. I slept a little but mostly just tried to stay warm.

Once again, I had to leave my shelter to find food. I headed out into the downpour. I was hungry, tired, and drenched. I left the shelter of the bush and stepped right into a mud puddle as deep as my chest. My feet and legs were now covered in sloppy mud. I tried to shake off the near frozen brown slop from my paws. First my back paws, then the front. One at a time, I shook them, but as soon as I put them back down on the ground, they were muddy and wet again. Oh, how I hate the rain!

I was out in the rain trying to find food, but the drumming of the rain on the ground masked any sound of mice rustling in the grass. I'm not going to be able to find food today, I thought. I turned to walk back to the bushes and saw three young boys out playing in the rain. Maybe one of them would take me home? I slowly crept up towards them not knowing if they would be friendly.

One of the boys saw me and said, "Hey look, a scrawny, dirty cat. Let's shoot him." All three boys turned towards me. In their arms, each one held a BB gun. All at once, they raised their guns. The hollow end of the barrels obscured their faces. I gazed straight into their weapons. I froze for what seemed like hours. I didn't know what to do. I'd so hoped they would be nice and take me home. I didn't want to believe they would hurt me.

Then I felt the sting as a BB hit me above my right eye. As the searing pain penetrated, I jumped and spun around. I sprinted as fast as I could away from them. Another shot pierced the back of my left leg, but neither BB slowed me down.

The mud and water splashed back up all over me as I ran for my life. I couldn't tell if it was blood or mud oozing down my forehead covering my right eye. My vision grew blurry. I don't know how long I ran. I just ran until I couldn't run anymore.

Too tired to continue, I stopped and looked back. The three juvenile delinquents were nowhere to be seen. I saw a bush nearby and scampered under it to check my wounds. I couldn't see out of my right eye. There was thick bloody mud dripping down my face onto the ground in front of me.

I lapped the mud off my paws then carefully wiped my clean, wet paws over my forehead, eyes, and cheeks. I was able to slowly and gently clean off the mud. I also cleaned most of the blood from my face. There was still some blood oozing from the puncture above my eye. The BB had penetrated too deep for me to pluck it out with my claws.

I let the residual blood drip down my forehead as I turned to inspect where the other BB had pierced my upper leg. I could feel the BB lodged in my muscle. The mud and blood had mixed to form a thick matted film down the entire back of my leg.

I lapped at the matted fur, removing as much of the mud and blood as I could. Around the wound, the blood started to harden. My fur formed thick-crusted lumps that I bit and tore at with my teeth. I pulled much of the fur off and licked the wound clean. I extended my claws slowly into the hole to try and remove the projectile. The pain built up slowly. At first it was a sharp stabbing. Then it progressed to a lightning bolt piercing my leg and shooting up my back. I nearly fainted and reflexively yanked my claw out of my leg. I'd better leave this BB alone also, I thought to myself.

Thankfully, the bush provided me some cover from the continuing downpour. Yet, I was weary, numb and drenched. To get out of the mud, I curled up on a small patch of leaves that had fallen from the bush. The rain falling on the surrounding shrubs now provided an almost soothing melodic lullaby that lulled me into a deep sleep.

I woke to a beam of warm, radiant light on my face. The sun penetrated the canopy above providing the first bit of warmth I'd felt in days. I tried to stand, but my back-left leg was achy, sore and stiff. I slowly stretched it out to loosen the muscle. The blood had dried on both my wounds.

The pain was subsiding in my leg and forehead. I thought getting out in the sun would be the best thing for me today. I crawled out from under the overhanging branches of the bush into the warm spring sunshine. For a while I just sat in the sun. It felt so warm, rejuvenating and soothing on my cold, tired body. The sun may have helped warm my cold body, but it did not fill my stomach.

I sat a little longer then headed out into the field to find something to eat. The sun was my friend. Its warmth brought out the mice. Within a few minutes I heard the first one rustling in the grass ahead of me. I stopped in my tracks and stood motionless. Then I heard it again!

Slowly, I lifted and lowered my paws. Gently I crept towards the sound of the mouse not wanting to make a sound. I heard it again, right in front of me. I tensed the muscles in my legs and released the springs. The leap was short but powerful. I landed right on the mouse.

It was trapped under my front paws but not in my claws. I had to be quick before it slipped out. I had to lift my paws to grab it with my mouth. As I lifted one paw, it slipped away. Quickly, I changed directions and pounced. Missed! I twisted to the left and lunged at the quarry. Missed again! A spin to the right and a swift swat with my paw pinned my prey to the ground. My head quickly followed my paw in one fluid motion. When the commotion ended, I stood tall with breakfast dangling from my jaws.

I caught three more mice in the same area. This was the place to be. I needed to find a good shelter nearby since there were so many mice. I didn't want to go far, but I had to look for shelter. All I found was a thick clump of dead sticks mixed with dried grass. Would this be a good enough shelter if it rained or snowed again? I pushed through the thick brush until I poked out of a thick clump of branches right into a small opening in the middle of the brush pile. Suddenly, I was not alone.

In the clearing were two large cats. They had been sleeping, but my careless noise woke them. One was a black and white cat like me but slightly bigger with much longer fur. His fur was wet and matted and splotched with mud from the storm. His eerie greenish-yellow eyes glared right at me.

Behind him was an even larger cat with no tail and massive paws. His fur was mostly brown. I couldn't tell if that was the color of his fur or if he was caked in mud. Both cats instantly jumped me!

The black and white one, being closer, was the first to sink his teeth in. He latched onto my right ear and shook his head. He ripped a chunk of my ear off. The other cat sank his massive claws into my back. I leaped as high as I could, doing a barrel roll in midair to shake him off. I landed behind the mud soaked brown cat and sank my claws into his rear end.

He shrieked and spun around. I swung my right paw, claws extended, across his face. My claws sank deep, drawing blood as they tore through his skin. My paw ripped fur from his face. He let out the loudest hiss I've ever heard and ran off.

Then I felt the teeth of the black and white cat sink into the back of my neck. He'd attacked me from behind mostly getting a mouth full of fur. Sadly, his teeth sunk deep enough to hold me with a tight grip. I rolled over, flipping him against the ground. Somehow it knocked him loose. As he fell away from my neck, he took a large clump of my fur with him. I had suffered too many injuries already these last couple days. Not wanting to suffer any more, I turned and ran back the way I came as fast as I could.

Once again, I was on the run. My ear was bleeding and burned with pain. I must have hit my head when I rolled to throw the cat off, as my right eye was throbbing and blurry again. I didn't think the cats were following me, but I took no chances. I ran until it got dark. I stopped by a small clump of short trees to provide some shelter if it started to rain again. The trees were open enough I could see and hear the cats if they had followed me.

BOOK 1: ME-NOW

I sat under the trees looking back. When I was satisfied they were not following me, I curled up and fell into a deep sleep. I slept deeper than I had ever slept before.

3

Four Angels

I don't know how long I slept. When I woke up my leg, head, eye and ear were all throbbing in pain. I had dried blood on my ear and was missing clumps of fur from my neck. Again, I could barely see out of my right eye. The sun was rising above the trees and felt warm on my sore body. It seemed as if every muscle in my body was tight, knotted or torn.

Today like most days, my stomach was empty. It growled louder than the two cats from yesterday. This morning it took longer than normal for me to stand up, shake out the knots and stretch my aching muscles.

I had no idea where I was. I had run so far the previous night that I ended up someplace I'd never seen before. I walked for hours looking for something to satisfy the gnawing in my belly. Eventually, I saw a few buildings in the distance. Buildings meant there were also people. So far, my experience with people had not been good. I didn't know what to do. Should I explore the buildings hoping there might be nice people to help me? Or should I go the other way and look for a safe place to hunt?

Then I smelled it. A deep heavy smell of meat and fire twirled on the breeze. I have never smelled anything like it before. One whiff, and I knew it was food. I had to find the source of that unbelievable smell, people danger or not. Slowly I followed the scent to where people were sitting outside a building eating. Was that smell coming from what they were eating?

Maybe someone would give me food. All I'd need was a little bite to lessen the aching in my stomach. I cautiously approached a person sitting alone. It was a large man who seemed to be eating rapidly. I wondered if maybe in his haste he would drop some food. Hesitantly, I crept under the table where he was sitting. He finished eating without dropping anything, not even a crumb.

I decided to make contact and ask for food. I rubbed my face against his leg urgently crying, "ME-NOW, ME-NOW, feed me now?"

The man kicked his leg out, knocking me to the ground and away from his table. He yelled, "Get out of here, you mangy cat!"

I ran off and hid behind the building until he left. Maybe the next person would feed me?

Two more people sat down next, a lady and a man. I slowly approached. Maybe she would be nicer? Again, I rubbed my head against her leg crying, "ME-NOW, ME-NOW, feed me now?"

"It touched me! That dirty cat touched me!" She shrieked in a high pitch that hurt my ears. Again, I ran off and hid until the couple left. Please, I thought, someone help me. "Feed me just a little," I wished. I was so hungry and too sore to try to hunt.

I waited behind the building and watched as other people came and went. After waiting for a little while, four people sat down at the same table. There was a young boy with short dark hair. With him was a short little girl with curly brown hair, large brown eyes, and a bright smile. Two other people sat down with the children. One was a tall man, the other a short woman with long brown hair. These four looked different than the other people who'd come and gone. They were smiling and talking softly to each other. I thought I also heard giggling.

They acted happy, and I thought if these people were not nice enough to feed me, nobody would. "Mommy look, a kitty!" the young girl chirped as she pointed at me.

"Oh, he looks so dirty and skinny," the woman said. She was older than the girl and taller but had a similar look with the same curly brown hair and beautiful smile. "He must be so hungry." She turned to the man, "Sweetie, hand me my burger."

"Here you go Angel," he said as he handed her something wrapped in paper.

She unwrapped it and broke a small piece off. She called softly, "Here kitty, kitty, kitty. Here kitty, kitty, kitty." She held a small piece of meat towards me.

"Oh, she was an Angel!" I thought. I ran up quickly, but stopped short of her wondering if this was real. "Was she going to feed me?" I slowly walked up, as she dropped the meat on the ground in front of me. It was delicious, the best I've ever tasted. I looked up at her, rubbed my head on her leg and cried, "ME-NOW, ME-NOW, feed me now!"

"Oh, he is adorable," she said as she dropped another piece of meat on the ground.

"Let's keep him mom!" the boy exclaimed. "He looks like he's a stray."

"I don't know. We have so many rescued cats at home already," the man said. "Maybe we should call the local rescue and see if they can help him?"

"Daddy we can't leave him here! Mommy, can we keep him!" the girl cried out.

"Your dad is right. We already have too many cats at home, and we can't save them all. I'll go get another burger for him so at least he will have something to eat," the Angel said. She stood up and went in the building. When she came out, she unwrapped another slab of meat and broke it into small pieces. Then she handed them all to me! She really was my Angel. After she fed me, the people got up and started walking away. The women paused and gave me a sad, somewhat guilty look as she got in the car. Then they drove away.

I was sorry to see them leave, but at least I had a belly full of meat now. I also knew some people would help and feed me. I had found a place I could find food. There were boxes behind the building for shelter. There were also bushes nearby to hide in if I needed to. I think I'll make this my new home.

With a full stomach, I explored the area until the sun started to set. The other buildings were empty. I found a place to curl up in one of the boxes behind the meat building to take a nap.

The next morning, I once again awoke to the warmth of the sun. The smell of fire and meat were once again wafting from the building. The sweet savor engulfed the air. "This would be a good home," I thought.

I slowly stretched and walked around the building looking for people to feed me. This time no one was sitting out at the table with food. The people walked from their cars into the building and back to their cars. Nobody sat at the table to eat. I sat and waited. It was hours before someone sat at the table. Like yesterday, some people screamed and kicked me away. Others gave me a little food. I was disappointed no one gave me as much or talked to me as nice as the family from the day before. I missed my Angel and her family. I wish they'd come back and feed me.

After I had a little to eat, I decided to see if there was any food at the other buildings. The first one had a lot of cars that would drive next to it and stop. A person would get out and stand next to the car, then get back in and leave. No one was eating. The smell in that building was horrible. I decided to move on and explore another building. Then I heard the angelic call, "Here kitty, kitty, kitty. Here kitty, kitty, kitty."

I turned and saw Angel and the young boy and girl by the meat building calling, "Here kitty, kitty, kitty. Here kitty, kitty, kitty." Angel was waving her hand near the ground. It looked like she had something to eat. I quickly ran over to them.

She handed me the food. Angel kept feeding me until I was full. I rubbed my head on her leg in appreciation. Then she bent over and picked me up.

"Why? What was she going to do?" I wondered. She walked with me to her car. The boy opened the door for her. Suddenly, she put me in a cage in the car. I didn't know why she would put me in a cage. She had been so nice to me, but now I was locked in a cage in her car.

We drove off and through the window I could see the trees whizzing by. I felt the swaying and rolling of the car. My head was spinning. My stomach felt uneasy. I'd thrown up hairballs in the past, but this time I threw up all the food she had given me. After I threw up, my stomach felt a little better. My head still felt like it was spinning. I curled up in the back corner of the cage. I wanted to be as far from the window as I could get. I didn't move until the car stopped.

4

I Hate Cats

The car door opened. Angel gently pulled the cage out and carried me into a building. She put me down on a shiny table and opened the door of the cage. The room was bright like a sunny day but without the warmth from the sun. There was a stale bitter smell in the air, unlike anything I had smelled before. I stayed in the cage, scared of what was out there.

"Hi doctor," Angel said as a tall man with short, grey hair on his head and his face entered the room. He was wearing a long white coat. He reached in the cage with very cold hands and pulled me out.

"Don't be scared little fellow. I won't hurt you," he said softly as he put me down on the shiny, hard table. Then he started feeling my body. He started softly closing his large hands around my legs and running his hand up and down each leg squeezing gently. Next, he slowly but firmly bent each joint in my legs. Then he pressed firmly on my feet to examine in between my toes. Afterward he ran his hands across my body firmly compressing my belly, almost lifting me off the table. He softly brushed through my fur with his fingers. He noticed I still had some dried blood on my fur.

The man took extra time in looking at the wounds on my leg and above my eye. A sharp jolt stung my leg as he pulled my fur aside and ran his finger over the wound on my leg. He pushed softly but firmly. I could feel the pressure on the BB still lodged in my leg. The sting caused me to jerk my leg away from him.

"I'm sorry little fellow. I didn't mean to hurt you," he said as he cupped my chin in one hand and held my head firmly. He shone a bright light in both eyes concentrating on my right eye. The light was so bright it burned my left eye. I struggled against his grip to turn my head away. When he shined the light in my right eye, I could only see a soft hazy light. It was not bright at all and did not hurt. All his squeezing was uncomfortable and hurt a little. Yet he constantly spoke in a soft calming voice and often stopped his exam to caress the top of my head.

"He needs some cleaning, vaccines and medication, but I think he will be fine," the doctor said.

"Oh, that's so good. You don't think he has anything serious, do you?" Angel replied.

The doctor continued, "No, I think he has worms and a bit malnourished. We can take care of those easily. It also looks like he has been in a fight. He is missing part of his ear. Also his right eye looks cloudy. I don't know if he can see out of it, but I don't think it will harm him. It looks like he may have been shot with a BB gun. He has what looks like a BB wound above his right eye and in his left leg. It doesn't look like they are in critical areas. The surgery to take them out would be worse for him than just leaving them alone. I don't think they will cause him any harm in the future. We'll get him cleaned up. You can take him home soon."

"Thanks, doctor. We'll be in the waiting room," Angel said in a soft almost tearful voice. "I'm so thankful he'll be OK."

The doctor poked me a bit more and stuck me in the rear end with sharp needles. He forced pills into my mouth and held my mouth shut until I swallowed them. I hated this. I think I'd rather be out in the snow than here. Yet, through all this the doctor spoke softly to me and gently petted me on my head or rubbed my belly. He held onto me with strong hands and would not let me go while he examined me. I felt an odd mix of fear and kindness. The doctor was gentle and caring.

The room's door opened with a slight creek. A young lady with long yellow hair, blue eyes and a soft but warm smile entered. She said, "If you're done with your exam doctor, I can clean him up."

"Thanks, I'm done. He could use a good cleaning," the doctor declared as he leaned over and kissed me on the top of my head. "You'll be fine little fellow. She'll take good care of you."

The blonde lady softly rubbed her hand over my head and down my back. "You'll be beautiful when I'm done," she told me.

"That's funny, I never thought of myself as beautiful, just cold and wet," I purred. She brushed my fur, tugging and pulling at the tangles and blood crusted fur. I wiggled and squirmed trying to get away. Finally she gave up the brushing and cut out all the mats and tangles.

"You're not going to like this little guy, but you really need a bath," she said in a soft comforting voice. Then she made it rain on me. I hate the rain. This rain was really weird too. It was a hot rain and soothed some of my aches and pains.

I thought to myself, "At least she didn't make it snow on me." She spoke softly and hummed while she made me cleaner than I can ever remember. When she finished my bath, I was warm and refreshed. I also smelled like flowers. The blonde lady put me back in the cage and carried me to Angel. Angel was waiting anxiously when the lady handed the cage to her.

"Thank you, he looks wonderful," Angel said with a big smile as she peered into the cage. Back into the car we went. I laid down waiting for the sick feeling. I shut my eyes and tried to sleep. While I slowly drifted off to sleep, I thought about what might be next for me. I was a little scared, but these new people had all been so nice to me. They seemed to want to take care of me.

I don't really like being locked in a cage, but at least it was warm and dry. The soft roar of the car and constant rocking eventually lulled me to sleep. I slept until I felt the cage being pulled out of the car. Angel carried me into another building. "Sweetie, we're home," she called.

"Hi Angel, how's the cat?" I recognized the deep firm voice. It was the man that was with Angel the first time I saw her.

"Hi Sweetie," Angel said. "He seems scared, but the vet said he was in good shape, mostly malnourished."

"Do you think he will get along with the other cats?" Sweetie asked.

"Cats! What other cats?" I screeched, but I don't think they heard me. Why would they bring me to a place with other cats? Don't they know cats will eat my food and try to hurt me, just like all the other ones did? I'll need to protect myself from them before they hurt me. My last encounter with cats cost me part of my ear and the vision in my right eye. I can't let that happen again.

Angel put the cage down, and two other cats slowly walked up to the cage door. I raised the fur on my back, pulled back my ears. Then I showed my teeth and hissed as loud as I could. I needed to make sure these cats knew I would not let them hurt me without a fight. They both hissed back but quickly ran off.

"Maybe we should put him in the basement alone until he gets settled in," Sweetie said with a concerned voice.

"Yeah, you're right." Angel responded. "Would you carry him downstairs, and I'll get a litter box and some food and water for him."

Sweetie picked the cage up and held it gently in both hands. He carried me downstairs and placed the cage on the floor. When they opened the cage door, both Angel and Sweetie were standing there looking at me. I slowly poked my head out. I carefully looked left then right. With no signs of other cats, I slowly left the cage.

I rubbed my head on Angel's leg, "Me-Now, Me-Now, feed me now," I cried. She bent down and put a bowl in front of me containing a soft, juicy mix of fish and sauce. I've never smelled anything this good. It was the most wonderful smelling food ever! Even the fire and meat at the buildings didn't smell this good.

"I gave him the seafood variety," Angel said to Sweetie. I'd never had seafood, but now I know, I love it! I ate until I couldn't eat any more.

I spent a few days alone in the basement. They fed me as much as I could eat. I could feel my strength returning to my muscles. This home was warm and dry. The other cats were upstairs. I could hear them and smell them, but they never came down.

The boy and girl would come down and play with me a lot. They often pulled a string attached to a fake mouse around the room for me to chase. I knew the mouse was fake, but it was fun chasing it. It also helped me keep my hunting skills honed. Sometimes the children would dangle a clump of bird feathers above me. I'd roll on my back and swat at them with both paws as if I was trying to knock a bird out of the sky. The kids would rub my head and stroke the fur on my back gently. They were good to me and often brought me extra food.

Then one day when Angel came down to feed me, one of the other cats followed her. I didn't see him at first, but when she put my food down, the other cat tried to steal it. I instantly jumped on his back and sank my claws into him. I hissed as loud as I could to let him know this was my food. That's all it took. He ran back up the stairs. Angel yelled, "Mickey, no!" and followed the other cat.

"Was she mad at me?" I wondered. "Mickey? Was I Mickey? Why would she be mad at me? The other cat was trying to steal the food she was giving ME." They were both gone, and Angel shut the door behind her. I settled down to another wonderful meal.

Every time one of the other cats snuck down to try and steal my food, I would immediately chase it off. I was not going to let another cat steal my food or hurt me ever again. Then one day Angel and Sweetie came down to see me. Angel picked me up. She held me close and rubbed my head. "Hey Mickey!"

"Mickey again?" I thought. I guess they are calling me Mickey now I liked the name.

"What are we going to do with him, Sweetie?" Angel said in a sweet but worried voice.

"I don't know Angel, but I am not sure we will be able to keep him if he keeps attacking the other cats."

"ATTACKING the other cats?" My ears perked up. Why would he say I am attacking the other cats? I was only protecting my food and myself. Those other cats were trying to steal food from me and might hurt me. Angel and Sweetie shouldn't keep the other cats. I protested with a soft meow.

"I know you're right Sweetie. It will be so hard to give him away."

"You'll find him a good home. You've found good homes for so many other stray cats you've rescued."

"I know, but Mickey is different. I need to find someone that I know will give him not just a good home but a great home. Maybe my brother wants a cat."

"Your brother lives in Vermont. How would we get Mickey to him?"

"My parents are going to visit him soon. Maybe they can take him."

"Vermont? What's Vermont?" I pondered. I hope they have seafood in Vermont.

5

Vermont

"We're going to miss you, Mickey. I'm sure you'll love Vermont," Angel said softly as she placed me in a crate in a car. "Take care of him mom and dad and have a safe drive." She said to two people in the front of the car as she closed the door.

I tried to sleep cooped up in the crate. The long day went on and on. In the front of the car was a man with grey and brown hair on his face and head. The hair on his face had tints of red. It seemed thicker than the hair on his head. He looked older than Sweetie with several creases in his face. He spoke on and off during the drive to a woman next to him, but the women did most of the talking.

She also was older than Angel and had long flowing hair. It was dark like the darkest night. They let me sleep and didn't bother me during the drive. The crate was large. I had plenty of room to stand up and stretch, but it still felt cramped. I lay in the pile of blankets Angel had left for me and tried to sleep. The blankets were soft and fluffy. I curled up tightly in them to try to muffle the constant groaning of the car. Sleeping was the only thing I had to pass the day. It helped keep me from getting sick. The car ride seemed like it would never end. We finally stopped. The two people in the front of the car got out.

"Mom, Dad, great to see you. How was the drive?" I heard a new man's voice speak from outside the car.

"Uneventful, as it should be," the woman from the car said. "Here's Mickey," she said as she gently pulled the cage I was in from inside the car. She handed it to the man.

A man and a woman peered through the holes in the cage door. The man looked similar to the man from the car, but the hair on his head and face did not have any grey. He did not have the same creases in his face either. I was apprehensive

31

about these new people but glad to be out of the car.

"Oh, honey, he's so cute, isn't he?" The woman standing next to him said. She had a warm, soft, caring face. She also had brown hair with a hint of red. Her pretty, brown eyes lit up as she saw me. She smiled.

"Yes dear," the man replied. "Let's get him inside and show him his new home."

We were standing outside of a different house. The sun was shining. It felt warm and refreshing. There was a slight breeze blowing but not enough to lift my fur. The breeze carried fresh air into my cage. I could smell flowers, grass, and clean crisp, but not cold, air. I thought I also smelled a mouse in the brush.

"This must be heaven," I sighed softly. "Why would I want to go inside, when it's heaven outside?"

They carried my cage in the house and set it down on the floor. Then the woman opened the door to let me out. I slowly tiptoed out of the crate, hopefully for the last time. I sniffed around for signs of other cats. There were none! Then "Yes Dear" put a bowl down in front of me. It was full of wonderful moist food, a nice treat after such a long car ride. I ate until it was almost gone, saving a little for later, just in case there was no more food.

I explored my new home thoroughly. I crept upstairs and downstairs. There were no signs of other cats, only me. "Was this new home to be all mine? Would I live here with Honey and Yes Dear forever?" I pondered.

My wish had come true! Vermont was a magnificent place to live. Honey and Yes Dear treated me wonderfully. They kept me well fed and gave me a warm, dry home to sleep in. There were no other cats. The house was all mine! Yet, part of me longed to be back outside in the sun and fresh air. I desired to go hunting again. What if these people stopped feeding me? I'd need to keep my hunting skills sharp and explore the area for the best hunting grounds. I sat in the window daily trying to decide where I would hunt if I got outside.

One day Honey and Yes Dear came to me while I was sitting on the windowsill looking longingly out the window at the grass and trees.

"Hey Mickey! Want to go outside?" Honey called.

"Does he really have to ask?" I thought. Of course, I want to go outside. I haven't known him that long yet, but I'm not sure he's the smartest person.

"Ok Mickey," He said. "You can go out, but we are going to have to put a harness on you and walk you on a leash. We love you and care about you. We don't want you to run away. We know you've missed being outside so much," Honey said as he picked me up and held me close to him. He rubbed his furry face on the top of my head. His face was as furry as I am. It was soft and soothing when he rubbed the top of my head. Then he kissed the top of my head and set me down softly next to the door.

"OK, here's your harness Mickey," Honey said as he wrapped a blue piece of cloth around my belly and neck. I heard a click as the buckle closed around me. Then he attached a rope to the harness. The harness pressed down on my fur. It wasn't too tight and didn't hurt, but it felt restrictive and confining. I had never worn anything like this. It was slightly uncomfortable. I crawled around on my belly trying to rub it off. It wouldn't budge. Finally, I stood up. If this harness was what it took to get me outside again, I was willing to try it.

Honey slowly opened the door. I slithered between his legs to get to the door. As soon as the opening was wide enough for me to squeeze through, I darted out towards the tall grass. "Slow down Mickey!" Honey blurted out as I sped away from him.

The rope attached to the harness tightened. The harness drew firm against my chest. In an instant and with a quick jerk, I was stopped in my tracks. The sudden stop almost knocked me off my feet. I made a quick recovery and sat up as if my movements had been intentional.

This wasn't a bad place to stop. I was in the midst of tall grass, moving softly in a light breeze. The air was crisp but not cold. The sun beat down on my black fur, quickly warming me up. The light breeze ruffled the short hairs on my ears causing a slight tingling sensation that perked me up even more than the warm sun. I sat for a moment taking in the warmth and smells of the grass and flowers that wafted on the breeze.

Honey took his time to catching up to me, letting me take in my surroundings. When he did catch up, he knelt next to me. Then he lightly patted me on the top of my head. "It's a beautiful day for a walk isn't it Mickey."

It took me a few days to really get used to the harness and leash. I tried to remember not to run too fast or the harness would jerk me back when I got to the end of the leash. I often was too excited to be outside and forgot about the leash. One day we were outside. I saw a bird in the grass. Immediately I went into hunting mode and slowly crept up to the bird. It was small, black and white with a short beak. The beak wasn't long enough to poke an eye out, so I wasn't worried. As I crouched slowly toward the bird, Honey stood quietly holding the other end of the leash that was attached to my harness.

As I got close to the bird, it suddenly noticed me and launched into the air. With two quick beats of its wings, it was off the ground and getting away fast. Instantly, I leaped toward the bird with my right paw and claws outstretch. My paw was descending on the bird's back when all of a sudden I felt a sharp jolt as the leash attached to Honey drew my harness tight. My leap toward the bird was halted in mid-air.

The sudden yank backwards just as I was leaping up started me tumbling upside down. There was no time to be scared. Instinctively I transferred my forward energy into the tumble giving me enough momentum to complete a full backwards flip, landing on my feet. As I hit the ground my knees flexed to absorb the fall. I stood unharmed but without my quarry.

"Are you OK Mickey? I'm sorry! I love you, but we like the birds too. I don't want you to kill them. You've plenty of good food inside if you are hungry," Honey explained as he picked me up to make sure I was unhurt. "We can walk wherever you want, but you'll have to stay close. We don't want you to run off and get hurt or lost," Honey continued as I started to squirm in his arms wanting back down. He finally got the message and gently placed me back in the grass.

"Let's walk down to the pond and see what's down there today. Does that sound good to you

Mickey?" From now on, I would hunt within the reach of my leash. I had a lot more freedom to hunt without the harness or leash. Sometimes I missed my early freedom of not having the harness, but if staying with Honey and Yes Dear meant having to wear it, I would gladly wear it. I quickly learned when they picked up the harness, it meant we would go outside. The buckles on the harness made a soft jingling when they lifted it up. I came running every time I heard it.

My walks with Honey and Yes Dear were my favorite times of the day. We would walk to a pond where I could hunt for frogs. Some days we would walk through the grass where I'd hunt mice. Other days we would walk to the woods. There I could hunt snakes. Snakes were harder to catch than mice or frogs. The snakes fought back, but they were worth the effort. They tasted great! No matter where we walked in Vermont, there was always good hunting.

My best days were when Honey would take me to the garden. The garden was full of all different sized and shaped plants. Some had small leaves and stood tall. Other plants flowed through the garden and had large broad leaves that provided wonderful shade on hot summer days. The garden also supplied plenty of snakes, frogs, and mice. I would hunt them all. After filling my belly,

I'd nap under the large leaves of the garden plants while Honey worked.

As the summer ended, cold winds and snow started. Honey started fires in the woodstove. The fires heated the entire house with soothing, dry warmth that helped me forget those early cold, wet days alone in the old wooden barn. I could sleep in front of the stove forever. Yet, I often left the warmth of the stove to enjoy the comfort of the bed with Honey and Yes Dear. I didn't like being alone. Usually I'd sleep on top of Yes Dear. Her warmth, soft heartbeat, and breathing were comforting for me. Being with her, I felt calm and safe.

My years in Vermont were wonderful. Then it happened. The house on wheels showed up. Honey and Yes Dear called it an RV. The RV sat outside for a while. I explored it when we went for our walks. I wasn't sure what to make of it. It was much smaller than our house. It had only one room with a few seats and a bed. The seats faced a big window so you could see outside. The RV also had an odd smell. It was a slightly damp, musty smell but also smelled a little like the car I came to Vermont in. The floors were cold. Worse, there was no woodstove to keep me warm.

Then the boxes came. Honey and Yes Dear started putting everything in the house into the boxes. One day we went for a walk to explore the RV and stayed. We stayed in the RV all night. The next day Honey and Yes Dear went outside but left me in the RV. At the end of the day, Honey came back and put the harness on me. He took me for another walk.

We went back into our home, but it was empty. There was no furniture, no bed, and no boxes. There were only empty rooms. We walked around for a little while. Honey and Yes Dear talked softly to each other. They seemed a bit sad about the empty house.

"Say goodbye, Mickey," Yes Dear said. "It's been a great home. We'll miss it, but the next one will be even better. I know you'll love it."

Then we went back to the RV to sleep again.

6

The Road

I sat in the back of the RV and stared out the back window as we drove away from our home. I was scared of what was to come. I didn't know it at the time, but that was the last time I would ever see my home in Vermont.

The days seemed to never end as we rolled down the road, day after day. We'd stop a few times every day. I would get a chance to go for a walk outside. Every night we would sleep in the RV. I always slept in bed with Honey and Yes Dear. I needed to make sure they did not leave me alone somewhere.

I hated the road, but at least I wasn't alone. I often remember those early days alone, before I found my home in Vermont. I wish I could forget those days, but the wind and snow always reminded me of the frigid nights alone in the barn.

I shiver every time I think about it. The damp musty smell of a rainstorm brings back the memories of my matted, soaking-wet fur covered in mud. Since finding Honey and Yes Dear, I haven't felt the gnawing cramps of having an empty stomach. I may be scared of what's to come, but I know Honey and Yes Dear will take care of me. They will keep me warm and dry and well fed too.

Each time we stopped the RV, we were somewhere new. Some of the new places were noisy with lots of cars and people. These new places were scary. I often stayed in our RV, cringing in the corner being too afraid to leave. Sometimes when we stopped, we would go for a walk where there were no people or cars. All I could see was grass and trees. I loved these new places. Sadly, our walks outside never lasted long enough. Too soon we were back in our RV.

A few days into our trip, we stopped in the middle of the day for a walk. Yes Dear gave me something to eat then started getting lunch ready for herself and Honey. While she prepared their meal, Honey took me for a walk. He put on my harness and leash then opened the door.

The air was cool but not too cold. The sun was not shining, but at least there was no rain. It was not a great day for a walk, but I wanted to get out and see the new sights. As I stepped out the door, I saw a large group of scary looking men. They were big men. All of them sitting on or standing next to two-wheeled vehicles. Some of the vehicles were running. They were loud and sounded angry. I stopped, not sure if it was safe to continue on our walk. As I stood at the door, Honey stepped out and called, "Come on Mickey. It's OK."

He's always protected me before. I trusted him and stepped out into the fresh air. We walked right past the group. I stopped and looked the men over. They stared back at me then looked at Honey. Honey just kept walking and calling me over to a grassy area with some trees. The men watched us walk by, but Honey never stopped. The two-wheeled machines growled loudly in the distance. I was afraid of them, but Honey didn't seem worried.

"Cute cat!" one of the men called. "Can I pet him?"

"Sure," Honey replied and stopped walking. The man was much taller than Honey. He had long, scraggly brown hair on his head and face. There was a scar under his right eye. I wondered if he got into a fight with a mean cat like me. The man was dressed all in black with heavy black boots that thumped when he took a few steps toward us. He knelt next to me and softly scratched behind my left ear.

"Nice kitty." He quietly spoke as he started softly stroking the top of my head. "What happened to his eye?" The man asked.

"We don't know," Honey replied. "He was a stray cat. When my sister found him, his eye was like that. The vet thinks he was in a fight, but he's doing fine now."

"He doesn't mind the leash?" The man in black continued.

"It took him a little while to get used to it. Now I think he's just happy to get outside," Honey answered.

"We're headed to Sturgis. Where you guys going?" The man asked as he stopped petting my head and slowly stood up.

"Moving to Alaska," Honey told him.

"Well, have a safe trip," The stranger exclaimed as he turned and walked back to his friends.

"Yeah, you too," Honey said as we turned and strolled to an area of bright green, chest-high grass.

I love fresh grass and stopped to eat a little before continuing over to scratch the rough bark of a nearby tree. My claws sunk deep into the tree trunk. Then I rhythmically pulled them back and forth. It felt good to exercise my nails, the rough texture curling between my toes. After a short walk, Yes Dear joined us. The two of them sat at a table and enjoyed their lunch. I lay down and waited for them to finish. When they were done, we walked back to the RV and continued on our way just as the rain started to fall. At least I didn't get wet.

We continued our drive day after day. I was thankful my nights were spent sleeping soundly, usually comfortably on top of Yes Dear. I wanted to make sure that if she got up to leave, I knew about it. Her warmth and soft, slow breathing were very comforting. The swaying motion of the RV became second nature after the weeks went by. I no longer felt sick to my stomach with the rocking of the moving house. I often walked around the RV looking out various windows to see where we were on our journey.

A few days later, we stopped for our mid-day snack and walk. Once again, Honey put on my harness and leash and opened the door. This time the wind was blowing hard. I hate the wind, but I wanted to get out of the RV and walk around. As I stood in the doorway, all I could see was grass. The land was flat. The grass stretched on for as far as I could see. If not for the wind, this could be a fun place. I hesitantly left the RV. Then I noticed a table where Honey started to head toward.

As we walked through the grass, hundreds of grasshoppers launched themselves out of our path. I sprinted to get in front of Honey. Without breaking stride, I leapt right into the cloud of fleeing grasshoppers. They were too fast and settled back to the ground beyond where I landed. They were just out of reach. Honey continued to walk and with each step grasshoppers soared into the air in all directions. I tried to stay in front of him so I could hunt before he scared them. Finally, he stopped and let me go ahead.

I crouched low. Slowly, ever so slowly, I inched one foot in front of the other. My steps were soft. I made no sound as I stalked my prey. All I could see was grass. My quarry was hidden deep within the tall wavy stalks. I took one step, then another. In an instant, hundreds flew out of my path. I leaped and tried to grab one in midair but missed and landed in the grass.

As I landed, hundreds more flew away. Every time I pounced, they flew away. I'd land and more would fly away. I got tired of pouncing and missing. I decided to sit and rest. As I did, Honey decided to continue to the table where he and Yes Dear would have their snack. As he walked, I noticed a pattern. A few feet in front of him, the grasshoppers would leap and fly off to either side.

I walked up until I was just in front of Honey. As he took another step, I leapt into the air ahead of him. As his foot came down, the grasshoppers took off. One jumped right into my paws. I held on and landed with my paw holding it fast to the ground. I extended a claw, and it stopped moving.

Now I could enjoy my snack while Honey and Yes Dear enjoyed theirs. I used to catch grasshoppers in Vermont, but these were larger and crunchier. They smelled and tasted a bit like the fresh grass they lived in. I caught two more before we left. Then we went back into the RV for another long ride.

That last stop was fun. There were so many grasshoppers for me to chase and catch. I've never seen so many. This has been a long trip in the RV, but each time we stop, we are somewhere new. Each new place has new sites, sounds, smells and new treats for me to try. This trip is not horrible. It's an ADVENTURE! I can't wait to see where we end up next.

The next stop was hot. I'd rather it be hot than cold, but this place was too hot. It was brutally hot. The sun beat down on my black fur. At first it was soothing and energizing. The longer I stood in the scorching sun, the more it started to burn. It was like sitting in front of a blazing woodstove for too long. There was no cooling breeze, just the blistering sun. We left the cool air of the RV and took a short stroll that took us around towering colorful rock formations.

There weren't many animals for me to hunt. There were no mice or grasshoppers and very few birds. While walking I realized why there weren't any other animals here. It was too hot, even for me. We walked for a little while but Honey and Yes Dear were hot also. We went back to the RV to have lunch and cool down. The air-conditioned RV cooled us off while Honey and Yes Dear made their lunch. They grabbed their lunch and a bowl of food for me. Then we went back out into the roasting heat. It was hotter than any of us would like, but we'd been cooped up in the RV too long. We found a wooden table under a large tree with broad overhanging branches to provide some cooling shade for us to enjoy our lunch.

We drove for another day, and when we stopped again, it was much cooler. This place also had a lot more animals. Some of these animals were the biggest I've ever seen. Many were even bigger than the bear I once saw back in front of our home in Vermont. We found a quiet spot to spend the night. Soon after we stopped, very large, hairy animals surrounded the RV.

"Look Mickey, bison!" Honey exclaimed as he pointed out the window at the giant animals waiting to trample me if I left the RV. I cowered in the window watching as these monstrous beasts went by. The RV shook back and forth as they rumbled past. I'm glad they weren't hungry. I think they could have smashed the RV with the horns on their heads.

"Don't worry Mickey. They eat grass not cats," Yes Dear calmly said. How did she know what I was thinking? The bison made their way past us and left us to a tranquil night sleep.

Our next day was like all the rest on this adventure. Most of the day was spent driving in the RV, but our choice of stops for the night was beautiful. I walked out the door of the RV and had to stop and take in the view. We were surrounded by the tallest trees I've ever seen. As a light breeze brushed the needles of the trees, it lifted the sweet aromatic scent of cedar through the air.

There were birds singing softly in the trees. Towering above the trees were snow-topped mountains. These were the tallest mountains I'd ever seen. The mountains in Vermont were tiny compared to these rugged peaks. The only thing I didn't like about this place was seeing snow. I hate snow. Although I had to admit, it looked pretty far away. I didn't think we would go for that long of a walk so I was all right with the snow being up there. We spent the night among the tall trees, surrounded by the majestic mountains.

The next day we drove through the mountains. We stopped a few times to walk among the trees along a beautiful lake. Later we decided to stay the night on the shores of that lake. While Honey and Yes Dear started to prepare dinner for all of us, I sat on the shores of the lake and listened to the lapping of the small waves on the gravely shore. I was mesmerized by the sound until something came into view.

It was the largest mouse I had ever seen, but it looked odd. It had a flat tail and was swimming in the lake. I hate water and wasn't going to try to swim to catch it. So, I sat behind some grass along the water's edge waiting for the giant mouse to come out of the water. Honey and Yes Dear sat at a table cooking their dinner over a small fire in a round pit. I am used to fires being in a metal box, like back in Vermont. This fire was outside and surrounded by rocks. It was warm, but I was scared to get too close to it without the metal box to protect me. The water mouse swam to the other side of the lake. Eventually, I decided to give up the hunt and see what Honey and Yes Dear had for dinner. Later, they told me the water mouse was a beaver.

We spent our days driving and each night we would stop and spend the night someplace new. I wondered if this was our new life or if this was just a wonderful adventure we were all taking together.

Once, we stopped but did not get out of the RV. I climbed up on Honey's lap and put my front paws on the front of the RV and looked out the front window. This was the most beautiful place we've been so far on this trip.

We were in a wide valley covered in large fields of bright green grass with scattered clumps of trees. The trees were mostly along the shores of a brilliant blue lake. Towering snowcapped mountains surrounded the valley. I wanted to get out and explore here, but we were stopped in a row with a lot of other RVs and cars. We seemed to be waiting for a lady with a sign on a pole. She walked up to talk to Honey. He opened his window to talk to her. "I see your license plate says Vermont! You're a long way from home," she said.

"Yeah, we're moving to Alaska," Honey told her.

"Well, welcome home. It's beautiful isn't it?" she said as she pointed to the mountains and the lake in the distance.

"It sure is!" replied Honey.

"What brings you to Alaska?" she asked

"Dogs. I want to get into dog sledding," he responded.

"DOGS! What does he mean dogs?" I panicked thinking about Honey and Yes Dear bringing dogs into my life. Honey's words brought back chilling memories I must have forgotten.

Before my angel rescued me, I had a few encounters with dogs. They were never friendly and always tried to attack me. If not for my speed and ability to climb trees, I might not have survived long enough to be saved. As I thought back to those horrible experiences with dogs, the RV lurched forward. The lady stepped back and waved goodbye. We made one more stop. Then our long road trip adventure came to an end.

7

Alaska

Alaska? Alaska. It even sounds exciting. The RV came to one final stop with me in it. Honey and Yes Dear opened the door for me. I stepped out into the warm summer sun. There was a cool breeze that washed the scent of the trees and grass over me. The high pitched but sweet melodic sound of birds singing filled the air while we strolled through tall grass. I know I heard mice rustling even if I couldn't find them yet. I think I'm going to like this place called Alaska.

We stayed outside for a little while and then went into what would be our new home. It was different than our last home. It was made from trees piled on top of each other. I walked around exploring my new home. I recognized the metal box in the big room, even without the fire inside. I knew when the nights got cold Honey would make a fire in the box to keep me warm.

We were all tired from our long trip. Yes Dear gave me a bowl of food while Honey made the two of them something to eat. After we all filled our bellies, Honey and Yes Dear sat and talked for a while. I climbed up on Honey's lap and relaxed while listening to their soft voices. I know they were both tired. It wasn't long before we all went upstairs for our first night's sleep in our new home.

The days were warm and long, and it never seemed to get dark. We could spend a lot of time outside exploring our new location. Fields of tall grass and stands of large trees surrounded our new home. One day Yes Dear said, "Honey, let's go to the beach and go clamming."

"Yes Dear, should we bring Mickey?" Honey asked.

"Sure, he'll love the beach," Yes Dear exclaimed.

We took a short walk to a place where there was sand and the largest pond I've ever seen. I could see the other side, but it was very far away. There were tall mountains on the other side. The waves were big and crashed on the sand sending a salty spray into the air that tickled my nose. I walked along the beach with Honey and Yes Dear. Every once in a while, they would stop and dig in the sand to pull something hard out of it. They called that hard thing a clam. The clams were long and skinny and smelled sweet and salty. I couldn't wait to taste them. "Dig faster!" I meowed.

They dug lots of clams. Then we returned home where they cooked a few for themselves and for me. "Wow, these are good. I don't even like clams," Yes Dear said to Honey.

"See, I told you these would be good. Mickey seems to like them also," Honey responded.

"Like them? I love them! They are the best clams I'd ever tasted." I looked up grinning. Oh yeah, they were the only clams I'd ever tasted. We would go to the beach and dig for clams a few more times that summer. We went until the air and water were too cold for us to be digging in the wet sand.

A few days after the trip to the beach, we went for another walk. This time we ended up along the shores of a fast-moving river to go fishing. Honey said the salmon were running, but I am pretty sure salmon swim. He's not very smart if he thinks salmon run. If he's right and they do run, I'm pretty sure I can run faster than they can. I'm gonna' catch one if it runs by me.

Honey used a long stick to toss a string into the river over and over again. There was a shiny piece of metal at the end of his string. "Mickey, this is the lure the guy at the store told me works best here," Honey explained to me. While I sat and watched him "fish," I also watched the river. The water was flowing fast, but it was shallow, hazy blue yet clear enough that I could see the rocks on the bottom. The shoreline was grassy with scattered clusters of shady trees.

I sat in the tall grass along the edge of the river. The light breeze rustled the grass but that sound was almost drowned out by the continual light murmuring, almost mesmerizing roar of the river. Then I saw it; the largest fish I'd ever seen! It swam so close to the grass that I'm sure I could have grabbed it. I moved closer to the water and watched closely for another fish.

Honey didn't see it, but I saw another one slowly swimming up the river towards us. I pawed at Honey's leg to try and let him know there was a fish swimming close. Honey looked at me and smiled, "I know Mickey. I'm trying to catch one for you." But he ignored the fish swimming towards us. If he wasn't going to catch it, I would.

I crouched low in the grass so it would not see me. Then slowly, oh so slowly, I moved right to the edge of the water. Just as it passed, I reached out and with claws extended swatted right at the fish. My claws dug into its back. I held on tight. As I dug my claws into the salmon, it thrashed its tail sending water splashing all over Honey and me. As the salmon tried to swim away, it dragged me into the river. I struggled to hold on as it thrashed about pulling me further away from the shore. I hate being wet! Now I was up to my neck in the river. "This fish better be good," I thought. "I don't care how wet I get. I'm not letting go."

Honey screamed, "MICKEY! I'll save you!" Honey dropped his fishing stick and grabbed the large net he'd brought. He swung the net at me. It landed on top of me. In one fluid movement, Honey flipped the net over, entangling both my catch and me. Honey pulled us back to shore, tossed the net and fish aside, grabbed me and held me tight. "Mickey, are you alright?" he said in an anxious shaking voice.

"Alright? I'm great! I just caught dinner!" I beamed as I looked at him.

"Look at that salmon, Mickey! It's bigger than you! You're the best fishing cat I've ever seen. Let's go home, dry you off and cook some salmon for you."

When we got home, Yes Dear dried me off while Honey cooked my salmon over an open fire. When he was done cooking, he gave me the first plate. Then they sat down to enjoy dinner. I've had seafood dinner before, but this was moist and meaty with a lightly salted scent. It was better than any canned seafood dinner I'd eaten before.

"Pretty good huh, Mickey?" Honey declared. "Nothing better than fresh Alaskan salmon."

One cooler day as the leaves of the aspen trees started to turn a bright yellow, Honey and Yes Dear decided to go on an adventure without me. They were loading what they called kayaks on top of the car. If they were going on a new adventure in Alaska, I wanted to go with them. While they put the rest of their gear in the car, I snuck out of the house and climbed up on the top of the car. I quickly crawled into one of the kayaks. I hid in the very front of the kayak, hoping they wouldn't find me. I really wanted to join them. I was stealthy enough not to be seen. Then they headed out for a short drive to a lake where they took the kayaks off the car. I stayed hidden as Honey sat in the kayak with his feet right by my face. I sat quietly for a little while then decided to see where we were and join the fun.

"Me-Now, Me-Now," I cried. "Let me up now!"

"Mickey! What are you doing down there?" Honey yelled. "How'd you get in there?"

I climbed up on his lap and poked my head out to see nothing but water. There was water and more water. Oh no, I'm not sure this was the right adventure for me. Instantly, I felt a little quiver in my stomach and noticed the rocking of the boat.

"Stay on my lap Mickey, you'll be fine. I won't let you fall in."

"How did he get in there?" Yes Dear asked anxiously.

"I don't know. Somehow he got into the kayak when we weren't looking. I guess he didn't want to stay home alone on such a beautiful day."

It was a beautiful day. We calmly paddled around the lake for a few hours then travelled along the shore among the lily pads. "Look Mickey, a dragon fly." It was a dazzling brilliant blue with four almost clear wings. It landed on Honey's shoulder and sat quietly. I was a little confused. Should I watch the beautiful dragonfly, or eat it? Before I could make up my mind, it flew off and landed on a lily pad. We sat quietly enchanted at its beauty until it slowly lifted off the lily pad. In a flash, it dashed off towards the shore.

I carefully climbed to the front of the kayak and crept out as far as I dared. There was a light breeze. The air was crisp and cool. It was wonderful to be out exploring. I just hoped I wouldn't fall in the lake.

Our summer continued into autumn with long sunny days of kayaking, clamming, and fishing. The days were getting shorter and cooler now. Each day there was a new adventure in our

Alaskan home. Then one day Honey started a fire in the metal box they called a woodstove. I knew that meant winter would be here soon.

I woke up one morning next to the woodstove. The fire had gone out sometime during the middle of the night. There was a slight chill in the room. Slowly I stood up, stretched, and decided to head upstairs. I jumped on the bed and climbed on top of Yes Dear. I knew she would keep me warm.

It was still dark when she woke up. She picked me up and gently laid me back on the warm bed where she had been sleeping. She walked to the window and peeked out. The full moon added a lot of light to the early morning darkness.

"Hey Honey, it snowed last night!"

"Snow?" I thought exasperated. I hoped we'd left that in Vermont.

Honey got out of bed and looked out the window. "Looks like we got a lot, maybe a foot." He went downstairs to restart the fire. Then they both got ready and headed out the door for the day. That was fine with me. With fresh snow outside, I decided to spend the day sleeping by the woodstove.

8

Dogs, Lots of Dogs

I awoke later that day to the sound of barking, lots of barking. It was close, too close. I didn't take the time to stretch out, but jumped straight to my feet and sprinted upstairs to hide under the bed. The barking continued, but it didn't get any closer. Slowly I crept out from under the bed. The sound seemed to be coming from outside. I leaped up on the windowsill to see what was going on and where all that barking was coming from.

It was a terrible site! Honey and Yes Dear were playing with dogs. Lots of dogs! Honey was walking to each dog with a large bucket. He scooped out what looked like soup. The dogs ate it ferociously. Honey gave them all seconds.

After the dogs finished eating, Yes Dear and Honey went around petting and playing with each dog. I shook my head side to side and couldn't believe my eyes!

I jumped down from the windowsill and ran to the door and waited for Honey and Yes Dear to return. The door slowly creaked open, and a burst of cold air washed into the house. The rush of winter air had the musky dank stench of wet dog.

The fur on the back of my neck stood up as I turned around and ran off sliding across the floor. My claws scratched the hard wood as I slid under a chair to hide. I peered out from the chair looking for the dog but did not see one.

"Oh no!" At that moment I realized the horrible stench was coming from Honey and Yes Dear. "Yuck!" That's disgusting, but at least there wasn't a dog with them. Their coats were covered in a layer of light fluffy snow. They shook off the snow before sliding their coats off and hanging them up to dry.

"Mickey, where are you?" Yes Dear blurted out as he scanned the room looking for me. "Oh, there you are! What are you doing hiding? We didn't bring any of the dogs in with us. They are outside dogs. Don't worry. The house is all yours."

I guess he thought that was supposed to make me fell better, and it did a little. Comfortable that there weren't any dogs with them, I poked my head all the way out from under the chair. I surveyed the room just to be sure. As I came out of my hiding spot, Yes Dear picked me up and held me tight, "Hey Mickey, we still love you. Did you see the dogs? They're sled dogs. Do you think you could pull a sled?"

"Yeah, right!" Honey exclaimed. "He barely goes out in the snow. Maybe he could pull a tiny sled with a mouse on back."

"He'd eat the mouse," Yes Dear chuckled.

That night I didn't sleep by the fire. I wanted to make sure Honey and Yes Dear stayed with me. I climbed up in bed and slept on top of Yes Dear all night. Before they fell asleep, they lay in bed talking.

"I can't believe we got such a great team of sled dogs!" Honey exclaimed.

"I'm so glad we were able to get Beans also, he's such a good dog," Yes Dear replied.

"Yeah, I know, a bit old but still a great dog. What about Gizmo and Griffin? Such good brothers, leaders and great runners," Honey continued.

"Don't forget their sister, Gracie, she gets so excited about running she almost goes nuts. Copper is a great leader also. I love the bear hugs he gives."

"Yes Dear, I do too but don't forget the other siblings Potter, Weasley, Bella and Draco. What a fantastic litter that is!"

"Oh, and Honey, what about Tinkle and Lil Moo? So small, but so much energy. All they want to do is run."

"And Munga, he's such a beast but so gentle, he could pull you up a hill by himself."

"Little cute Daisy really seems to like Nikko, doesn't she?"

"Yes Dear, Nikko seems to like her also, such great dogs. I also love how such a shy, sweet dog like Daisy runs with so much energy with her tongue hanging out like Michael Jordon."

While they talked, I laid quietly on Yes Dear listening intently to the conversation. The entire time, Honey lay on his side facing Yes Dear and me. He softly stroked my back with his hand. Occasionally, Honey would lean up and give me a gentle kiss on the top of my head. Their gentle caress and kisses seemed to prove they still loved me even with all the excitement about the new dogs.

That night, the moon cast light through the window across Honey's face. I could see he was smiling as he fell asleep. He must be happy with the dogs, or maybe he is happy with me. Probably a bit of both I decided. Well, if dogs make him happy, maybe they aren't all bad. I don't trust those dogs, but maybe I should give them a chance and see what they are all about.

As the winter continued, I watched from the window as Honey and Yes Dear put harnesses on the dogs. They'd clip them to long lines in front of wooden sleds. Then they would take off down the trail and be gone for hours. They never took me on these adventures but always left me with a nice fire burning in the woodstove. I was warm and comfortable inside.

Every time they returned home, I would meet them at the door. After they removed their snow-covered coats, they would pick me up and hold me tight. Yes Dear would always give me a loving kiss on my head and then softly rub it. Sometimes she gave me a tender scratch behind the ear. Honey had his own way of greeting me. He would gently rub his furry face on the top of my head. It felt warm and soothing. I pushed my head against his chin and rubbed him back.

Thankfully they never brought the dogs inside. The dogs always stayed outside. I still got to sleep by the fire or in bed, whichever I chose. I was scared of the dogs, but every time Honey and Yes Dear left, I wondered how much fun dogsledding might be. These were adventures I was missing.

I knew if I tried to go with them, the dogs might attack me. I also knew I could handle myself against one dog, but there were too many of them outside. I wouldn't stand a chance against so many.

One morning Honey went out and fed the dogs as he did every day. Only this time, he came right back inside. He knelt down and rubbed my head. "The dogs get a day to rest today. Do you want to go for a walk with me Mickey?"

"You know he hates the snow," Yes Dear reminded Honey.

"Yeah, I know, but he's been so adventurous since we got to Alaska. I thought he might want to explore the Alaskan winter."

"Yes, I am adventurous! I do want to explore the Alaskan winter. I think I'm ready for a walk in the snow." I thought as I strutted over to the back door. "Me-Now, Me-Now, Take me out now!"

"I guess he does want to go for a walk. OK Mickey, let's go."

The snow was cold and wet on my feet, but the sun felt warm on my fur. It was quiet outside, no birds singing, no grass blowing in the wind. Even though I loved those sounds, the quiet of the winter was peaceful. That peace was broken when the dogs spotted me. They went crazy, running around and barking at me. I turned and sprinted back to the door. Honey picked me up. "Don't worry Mickey. They won't hurt you. I'll protect you."

I know he's always protected me in the past, but this time I think I'll go inside just in case. I scratched at the door anxiously. Honey let me back inside.

Later when Honey or Yes Dear would take me for a walk, I would venture closer and closer to the dogs. They always barked and ran around wildly but never chased after me. On one of my walks, I got close enough to realize they were tied up with a metal rope. This meant I could get closer to them, but they couldn't get any closer to me. If they can't get closer to me, then I can get as close to them as I want. I decided to try it out. I walked up to the closest dog and stood just outside of his reach.

"Wow Mickey, you're getting brave," Honey said as the closest dog barked and jumped in an attempt to reach me. He was a large dog that came up to Honey's waist. His head was large and blocky. His silvery white fur covered a muscular stocky body with thick long legs. He had a distinct black spot of fur under his left eye that was shaped like a hook and made it look like he had a scar. His barks were rough, short bursts of almost defining thunder. With each bark, his long sharp fangs were exposed as a small amount of saliva dripped from his lower lip. He was the toughest meanest looking dog I've ever seen.

My skin tingled as the fur on the back of my neck stood up. I felt a little apprehensive, but I also felt safe with Honey next to me. I guess I WAS brave.

"Nikko be good. Mickey is just trying to be friends."

I just sat for a while watching Nikko bark and jump. I didn't think he'd ever stop as long as I was sitting in front of him. Then without notice, he lunged forward towards me. I knew he couldn't reach me, but my reflexes kicked in. Instantly I extended the claws on my right paw and sliced them across Nikko's nose. He let out a horrific screeching yelp. It was louder than that cat I beat up years ago. Nikko jumped back, ran into his doghouse and whimpered softly.

"Mickey, that wasn't nice. Are you alright Nikko?" Honey went to check on Nikko. "You'll be fine, Nikko. Just a bit of a cut on your nose. That'll teach you to mess with Mickey."

"Yeah, that'll teach you to mess with me! Any of you other dogs want to feel my claws? I got enough for all of you." I let them know I was the boss as I swished my tail in the air. I was tougher than they thought I was. Slowly I made my way around to all the dogs. Honey introduced them to me one at a time. Some of them seemed to want to play with me. Others I think wanted to eat me. The ones that acted like they wanted to eat me got a swat across their noses just like Nikko.

Finally, one by one, they all realized I was not their dinner. This was my home first. If they were all going to live here, they needed to know I would fight back if they tried anything.

Lastly, we stopped at the house of an older looking dog. He was calmer than the rest. "Mickey, this is Beans. Beans, this is Mickey," Honey said by way of introduction. Beans was not the largest dog outside, but he was big, stocky and had long dark fur speckled with streaks of grey. He was an impressive looking dog, even to a cat. Beans radiated confidence. Later I found out he had good reason to be confident. I heard Honey and Yes Dear talking about his career as a sled dog. He'd finished every race he ever started and ran the 1,000 mile Iditarod race to Nome four times! His leadership skills showed, as he stood tall over me. He didn't bark at me. He just bent over and sniffed me a couple of times. I had a feeling he wouldn't hurt me, and I stepped closer.

"Beans be good!" Honey exclaimed as he knelt next to the two of us. I think Honey wanted to be close just in case Beans was going to try something mean. I took another step forward. As I did, Beans lunged towards me, his mouth open wide. I froze. Instead of his teeth, I felt the cold wet sloppy tongue of a dog. That dumb dog licked me across the face and left slobber dripping from my nose! It was one of the most disgusting things I've ever felt! But at least it wasn't his teeth. I guess it was Beans' way of telling me he thought I was his friend and not his dinner. Either way, I didn't like it. Not one bit.

A few days later, I went out with Honey. He was "taking care of the dogs," which mostly meant scooping up their poop. It was a cold day. I decided to head back toward the house to go inside and warm up.

"GIZMO, NO!" Honey screamed. I turned to see Gizmo, a black and white dog who was thin and sleek streaking toward me at a full out sprint. He looked crazy! Honey dropped the scoop and turned to chase Gizmo. I knew Honey could never catch Gizmo before he got to me. I didn't have time to think. I was too far from the house and too far from the closest tree. Gizmo was moving lightning fast.

To make myself look bigger, I turned sideways. I hunched my back up tall and all my fur stood straight on end. I held my tail as high as I could hold it, my ears back. Then I hissed as loud as I could. My claws came out ready to strike him as soon as he got close enough, which didn't take long. When he was just about in range, I raised my front paw, ready to strike. Suddenly, Gizmo leapt over me and landed behind me. I spun around quickly. As I did, I swung my paw across what should have been his nose, but he leaped again, back over me. Once more that crazy dog landed behind me. Instantly I turned around again to face Gizmo who was now standing with his head down, his butt up in the air. His tail was wagging. He was yapping at me, not barking or growling but a playful yap. He bounced up and down running around me.

Not quite sure what to make of him, I decided not to take a chance. When he came closer, I bit down on his wagging tail. He yelped and started to run away. I chased after him furiously. He didn't run far before he spun around, rear paws sliding in the snow. When he stopped, he was once again facing me and wagging his tail. Yet again, he lowered his head and yapped at me.

Now I knew Gizmo was playing with me. Oddly, I think he thought I was playing with him too. Well, playing with him is a lot better than being a snack for him. I decide I would play. We ran around the yard, chasing each other while Honey chased us both. Honey was way too slow to catch us. Gizmo and I took turns chasing each other. I got in a few more bites on his tail just for the fun of it too!

Gizmo had a lot more energy than me. I grew tired first and stopped chasing him, which made him stop running. Then he gave me a big lick across my back just as Honey finally caught up to us. Honey seemed shocked that I was still alive. "Good boy Gizmo, GOOD BOY!" Honey exclaimed while he gave Gizmo and then me a long hug. Honey let me in the house then took Gizmo back to his.

After that day, I knew I had free run of the dog yard. The dogs were friends, not enemies. Some of the dogs still seemed a little uneasy letting me roam through the yard, but they never bothered me. Most of the dogs wanted to play with me, that is when they weren't going for a run. They loved to run. Beans seemed too stoic to play but always greeted me by lapping his big wet tongue across my face.

9

Learning to Mush

Honey and Yes Dear spent most winter days dogsledding. I'd watch them from the window until they were out of sight. Then I'd make my way to the woodstove and sleep the day away until I could hear the dogs barking again upon their return.

Some days Honey would go dogsledding without Yes Dear, and she would stay home with me. One of those days, Yes Dear was getting ready to go out and help Honey hook up the dogs. I decided to go out and help also. I think I know why Yes Dear decided to stay home today. It was COLD! But I was determined to go out and help. I supervised Honey and Yes Dear as they put the harnesses on the dogs and hooked them up to the gang line in front of the sled.

I also checked each dog before he or she got a harness on to make sure he or she was ready to go. They always were. It was taking Honey and Yes Dear a long time to hook up all the dogs. Waiting on them, I began to shiver. I figured I'd crawl inside the sled bag where I could get out of the cold for a moment while I waited. There was a lot of stuff in the sled bag including a soft fluffy sleeping bag. It looked like a good place to get warm, so I climbed inside. I curled up in the sleeping bag and waited for Honey and Yes Dear to finish hooking up the dogs.

I guess I must have dozed off, because I awoke with a jerk as the sled lurched forward. Then it started speeding down the trail. I stayed hidden in the sleeping bag for a while, not sure what to do. Eventually, I decided to poke my head out and see what was going on. The sled was moving pretty fast down a trail through the woods. The dogs were all lined out in front of the sled running hard. Yet, they looked almost effortless as they ran. I sat up straighter, my head poking out of the sled bag, mesmerized by the dogs.

Their feet and legs worked in unison, heads all forward and tails down. What was most surprising to me was that all the dogs were quiet, really quiet. There was no barking, no yapping... just the sound of the sled quietly sliding over the snow with the light jingling of the dog collars. I was surprised how quiet it was until... "MICKEY! What in the world are you doing in there?" shouted Honey.

I glanced up at him thinking how stupid his question was. Obviously, I'm sitting in the sled watching these beautiful dogs run.

"I didn't see you climb in there. You must be freezing."

Oh yeah, I was cold, but the hypnotizing motion of the dogs and the beauty of this winter wonderland almost made me forget I was cold. I wished Honey hadn't reminded me. He'd broken my trance. Now my nose and ears started to feel the stinging cold. The wind from us moving so quickly forward made it worse. My whiskers felt heavier now as the breath from my nostrils froze in place on them.

"Mickey, it's below zero! We'll turn around as soon as we can and get you home," Honey exclaimed in a soft but concerned voice. We continued down the trail a little longer. "Gizmo, Griffin, let's go home. Gee, Gee!" Honey called to the dogs. Gizmo and Griffin, in lead, without hesitation turned right, down a new trail. "Gee, Gee," Honey called again, and they once again turned right. One more time with the right turn then, "Haw, Haw, let's go home guys," he called. The dogs turned left in unison back onto the trail we started on. We had turned around and were now heading back home.

"That was amazing!" I mused. Just calling "Gee" or "Haw" made the dogs turned right and left. They understood Honey. I thought only I could understand him. I didn't know dogs were smart too. Well, I decided, they might be smart, but not as smart as cats. Soon, we arrived back home. Yes Dear heard us coming and was waiting for us outside. I was riding proudly on the sled and smiled at her.

"Mickey, there you are! You scared me. I couldn't find you anywhere."

"Of course you couldn't find me, I was dogsledding," I thought for a moment then wondered if the dogs might be smarter than the humans. She grabbed me, pulling me out of the sled and into her warm coat.

"Take him inside and warm him up. I'll take care of the dogs," Honey told her. Yes Dear carried me back in the house. We both sat by the woodstove and warmed up. Now I understand why they moved us all the way to Alaska. That was fun! Man, I can't wait to go again!

The next day was not as cold. I decided to try dogsledding again. This time I was going on purpose. I went out to help hook up the dogs. When they were just about ready, I hopped up on top of Honey's sled and waited to go. Honey brought the last dog to the sled and hooked him up. When he saw me sitting on the sled, he picked me up and put me to the side out of the way.

"Mickey, didn't you learn your lesson? You can't go." As he walked to the back of the sled, I hopped back up. "Mickey, what are you doing?" He stepped off the back runners to come take me off again. As he got to me, the sled surged forward. The dogs were tired of waiting and wanted to get on the trail. The sled was tied to a tree. Both snow hooks were dug deep into the snow, but the sled surged again. The rope and hooks strained to hold the sled back against the strength of the dogs.

Just as Honey bent down to pick me up, the sled surged one more time. This time the rope snapped! Both hooks ripped from the snow. Suddenly, the sled rocketed forward. Honey missed grabbing me. Instead, in smooth motion he spun around and grabbed the handle bar of the sled as it flew by. He was yanked off his feet but held onto the handlebar. In one graceful motion, he swung his feet around the back of the sled and onto the runners. If I had to guess, I'd say it looked like he'd done that before.

"Well Mickey, I guess you're going with us." Honey said exasperated.

"Of course I'm going." Why does he think I jumped up on the sled? Now, I'm really thinking he's not that bright. The dogs knew I was going.

What a day we had. It was my first full day dogsledding. It was so peaceful. The beauty of the surroundings was more than I had ever seen. I didn't mind the cold. I was too busy enjoying the day to notice it was a colder day than any cat should be out in. But I'm not any cat. I'm Mickey, the Mushing Cat!

Most of the day was quiet except for a few moments when we were speeding down a hill or around some tight turns. At one point we stopped at the top of a hill. I could see tall mountains in the distance. The sky was clear and brilliant blue. "Beautiful day, huh Mickey?" Honey asked as he stomped on the two hooks to drive them into the snow.

I wondered if that would hold us this time. Then Honey opened the sled bag, pulled out a small bag, and walked up to the dogs. He gave each of them a short pat on the head as he walked to the leaders. Today that was Copper and Bella. Honey gave them both a hug and kiss then pulled out a chunk of salmon from the bag and tossed a piece to both of them. As he walked back to the sled, he tossed a chunk of salmon to each dog. When he got to me, he broke off a smaller piece and handed it to me. "How about you Mickey, want a snack?"

"Salmon? You bet!" Now I know he's not that smart. Since when have I ever turned down salmon? Why'd he even ask?

Honey pulled a snack for himself out of his jacket pocket. We all enjoyed our snack and the view. The dogs seemed to eat their snack in one quick bite while Honey and I savored ours, staring at the mountains in the distance. The dogs got tired of waiting for us and started barking and leaping, driving hard into their harnesses. The lines attached to the snow hooks tightened. The dogs decided it was time to get moving again so Honey stepped onto the runners.

"You guys ready?" He said as he leaned over and pulled the snow hooks out of the snow. "Alright, let's go!"

The dogs took off again, with almost as much enthusiasm as when we started the run. We were out for a while longer. I enjoyed every minute of it! When we made it back home, the dogs and I once again enjoyed a salmon snack. Then I went inside to enjoy the warmth of the woodstove. We would go dogsledding almost every day. There were some wonderful runs. Some of the runs were quiet and peaceful. Others were very exciting and at times a little scary.

10

Dog Sledding's Not So Hard

"Hold on Mickey! This is going to be fun!" Honey exclaimed as he jumped off the sled. He started running behind the sled, pushing it up the hill. "Ready guys? Let's go!" The dogs drove forward as Honey pushed. We slowly made our way up the steep hill. The weather had been cold and sunny for the last week with no fresh snow. The trails were hard packed and slick. Snow crunched and squeaked under the force of Honey's boots. The runners swooshed softly as we crept slowly toward the top of this hill.

There's no need for me to hold on for this. I wonder if Honey ever knows what he's talking about. The lead dogs crested the hill and began picking up speed as they descended the other side. The rest of the dogs followed and dropped out of view over the crest of the hill. As more and more dogs disappeared, we sped up faster and faster. Swiftly, the sled reached the top of the hill. Honey jumped back on the sled and shouted, "HERE WE GO!"

Hold on was right! I drove my claws into the canvas of the sled bag as deeply as I could. The sled picked up speed fast. We rocketed down the hill.

"Easy dogs, easy!" Honey called, but the dogs were not going easy. They kept moving faster and faster. I could tell they loved speed. The sled slid to the left side of the trail. There was a sharp jolt as we bounced off a snow bank along the edge of the trail. The sled rattled from the force of the collision with the snow bank. I felt it tremble beneath my feet. My claws dug in deeper as I started losing my grip. We then made a sharp right turn, then back to the left. The back of the sled fish-tailed from side to side as Honey jumped from one runner to the other trying to maintain balance and control of the sled.

My rear legs slid back and forth in rhythm with the sled as I lay on my belly and clung on with my front claws. The force of the wind flattened the fur on my face and pushed my ears back. My eyes started watering. I felt a little queasy as fear welled up inside my stomach.

We continued down the hill and were moving fast. The trail turned sharply around a tree. The dogs hugged the edge of the trail and cut close to the tree. As the front of the sled approached the tree Honey jumped off and held onto the handle bar. His legs flailed franticly as he was trying to keep up with the dogs. He seemed to be taking giant steps, struggling to remain upright. As he did this, he tilted the sled up on one runner and shoved the back end of the sled away from the tree. I clung onto the sled bag for dear life! My front claws sank hard into the bag as my back legs slid off the side of the sled. I felt them brush the top of the snow on the trail. A cold chill went up my spine.

Honey was now pushing the sled towards the other side of the trail near a steep drop off. As we rounded the turn, he lowered the sled back onto both runners and jumped back on. He tapped the break with his right foot. The back of the sled hesitated as the force of the dogs yanked the front of the sled the rest of the way around the tree. We were now in the center of the trail.

My back legs were still dangling over the side of the sled bag. Honey reached around the side of the handle bar, tucked his right hand under my legs and nudged me back on top of the sled. I repositioned myself just in time for another steep drop. After that, we leveled off onto a flat smooth trail. The dogs slowed as the trail leveled out.

"That was fun, huh Mickey?" Honey asked his voice shaky.

"You know what? That was fun! I want to do it again." I smiled at him. This dogsledding's not so hard.

The day continued with a few more hills, but mostly we had relatively level and easy trail. The sun continued to shine brilliantly in a cloudless sky. Sadly, this time of year, it did not provide much warmth. When the cold became too much for me, I climbed inside the sled bag to warm up. Honey always kept a warm blanket inside the bag for me. The gentle rhythmic movement of the sled lulled me to sleep. After a short nap, I climbed back out on top of the sled to see how my dogs were doing. I soon learned, I'd checked on them just in time.

As I settled down on the front of the sled, we dropped down a short hill onto a frozen lake. There was no snow on the lake, just ice. The trail turned sharply to the right as we hit the ice. The dogs followed the trail, but the sled slid sideways off the trail. It was headed directly towards the center of the lake. Just off the edge of the trail, the sled runners hit a stick frozen in the ice. The runners suddenly stopped sliding, but the momentum of the sled caused it to flip over on its side. I held on tightly! My front claws gripped the sled bag as hard as I could. My back legs were dragging on the ice. Now that's cold! I kicked my back legs until I was able to get my rear claws into the sled bag. Eventually, I clawed my way up onto the side of the sled.

The dogs were running faster now that the ice provided little resistance. I turned around to see Honey holding onto the handlebar with one hand. He was being dragged face down on the ice. His other hand was trying to grab hold of the metal hook that was clanking and bouncing on the ice in front of him. Finally, he grabbed the hook and tried to dig the points into the ice as they scrapped along the solid lake. Fine flakes of ice sprayed up from the claws of the hook into Honey's face.

"Whoa, WHOA!" He yelled until the hook finally caught on a crack in the ice. The sled slammed to a halt. My body lurched forward suddenly. My claws sunk deeper in the bag, and I held on tight.

Honey slowly stood on the slippery ice trying to raise the sled upright and back on the runners. I climbed along the side of the sled and back onto the top as he straightened it. Just as he lowered the sled back onto the ice, the hook gave way. The dogs took off again. Honey slipped on the ice. Holding on tight to the handle bar, he flipped the sled onto its other side as he hit the ice again.

This time I could not hold on. I hit the ice, feet first of course. I can't say the same for Honey. I think he hit face first again. The sled slid past me, as I stood helpless on the ice. As Honey slid by, holding onto the sled with one hand, he scooped me up with the other. In one swift motion, he lifted me back up on the sled. He was still being dragged facedown. This time the hook was stuck under the sled. There was no way for it to catch on the ice. Honey could do nothing but lay there screaming, "Whoa Gizmo! Whoa!" "Whoa Griffin! Whoa! WHOA! WHOA!"

The dogs didn't listen. They were having fun. You know what? Secretly, so was I. The louder Honey screamed, the faster the dogs ran. Finally, he stopped screaming and just lay on the ice. He was still holding on, dragging quietly behind the sled, waiting for the ride to stop.

"But when would it stop?" I wondered. If the dogs wouldn't stop when Honey asked them to, when would they stop? I was worried now. This was fun at first, but now I wondered where we would end up. We took another sharp turn. The dogs left the ice of the lake returning to the snow-covered trail. As the sled, still on its side, hit the snow on the trail, the sled and dogs came to a stop.

Honey found the hook and jammed it into the snow. He then lay on the ground for a little while. I hoped he was all right. I knew the ice was hard and cold. Honey slowly stood up, brushed some snow off his face and chest then grabbed his elbow. He moved it back and forth a few times and asked, "Are you OK Mickey?"

"I'm fine. I'm not the one that was dragged on my face across the ice," I thought.

He walked over and picked me up and patted my head. "You look like you are having fun. Glad you're OK." He pulled the sled up with one hand while he held me with the other. He placed me gently back on top of the sled. Then Honey rearranged the hooks in the snow to make sure they would hold. There was one on the left and one on the right.

Honey opened the sled bag and pulled out a bag of salmon treats. He limped gingerly up to the leaders, Gizmo and Griffin, hugged them and patted each of them on the head before tossing them both a salmon treat. He continued down the line of dogs, rewarding each one with a treat.

I thought he would be mad at them since they didn't stop when he hollered, but as he tossed them the salmon, he patted each one and said, "good dog, good dog." When he finished giving the dogs a treat, he gave me my salmon treat also. Honey watched as I ate my treat.

"My mistake Mickey. I knew we hit that ice too fast, and we'd slide and flip over," He continued to explain. "Once we dumped over, I knew I had to stay calm. But, I was worried you might be hurt. The dogs respond to the tone of my voice. The louder I screamed, the more excited they got. I should have stayed calm, and maybe they would have stopped sooner." After we all finished our snack, we got moving again and headed home. I am sure Honey was happy to get home to a warm fire and a warm meal. I know I was.

The next few years were very similar. We spent our summers fishing, clamming, and kayaking and spent the winter's dogsledding. Sometimes Honey and Yes Dear would pack up the truck with the sleds, their gear, and the dogs and go away for a few days, leaving me home. The boy next door would come over to feed and play with me while they were away. He was always very nice and took great care of me, but I didn't get to go outside.

These times were very lonely for me since I didn't have Honey and Yes Dear for company and because I couldn't get outside and spend time with Beans or the other dogs who stayed behind. Each time Honey and Yes Dear left, they would take different dogs. Yet, it seemed like Beans was always left at home, just like me. He always had company, but I felt bad he never went on the trips with the others.

Honey called him, "Old Man Beans." Maybe he was too old to do whatever they were doing on the trips.

Every time Honey and Yes Dear came home, I would greet them and get a warm hug from each of them. Then I'd race out to greet the dogs. Beans was always the first dog I would visit. I'd snuggle up against his big furry chest, as he'd rub his cheek on the top of my head before dragging his soggy, warm tongue across my face.

Then I wondered, "if Beans was too old to go on the trips, why did they leave me home? I was not that old, and I didn't have to run." I wanted to go on those adventures with them too. After all, that's why we moved to Alaska. I decided that I wasn't going to be left home alone anymore. If they wouldn't take me, I'd sneak out and hide in the truck or sled to go on the next adventure with them.

Each time they loaded up the truck and went on an adventure without me, I tried to sneak out and hide, but either I could not get out of the house, or they would find me hiding in the truck. One day we were all out in the yard. I was supervising Honey and Yes Dear filling a lot of bags with gear and food. There were a LOT of bags with more dog food and treats than I've ever seen before. I knew this next adventure was going to be a big one. I had to find a way to join them. I was tired of missing the fun.

11

The Iditarod

Honey picked me up and gave me a kiss on the top of my head. He held me tight in his arms and rubbed my head with his furry face for a little while. I brushed my head back against his chin. It was fuzzy and soft and soothing against the top of my head. "I'll see you in a couple of weeks Mickey. I'm going to miss you," he said softly with a slight quiver in his voice. A single tear rolled down the side of his nose. He kissed me again then handed me to Yes Dear.

"Don't worry Mickey. I'll only be gone a couple of days," she reassured me then set me down on my mat by the fire. I sat silently by the fire while I watched the two of them haul a couple large bags to the door. Then I slipped quietly around their legs as they stood next to the bags.

The top of one of the bags was open. While Honey and Yes Dear were giving each other a long hug, I crawled inside to hide without them noticing. It was large enough that I could shimmy under the clothes inside. The bag lifted off the ground and bounced off Honey's leg as he lugged it outside. When he placed it back on the ground, I waited a moment then poked my head out the top, hoping they would not see me.

The bag had been left next to the truck. A light snow was falling now. The truck had a thin coat of dry fluffy snow. It also had dog boxes on the back with the sled on top of the boxes. When they left on their adventures without me, they always had the dog boxes with one or two sleds on top. This time I was going on the adventure with them.

I scurried out of the bag, bounded up the truck bumper and onto the hood almost sliding off since the snow caused the truck to be slippery. I was slipping and sliding, having trouble making headway as I rushed to get to the sled before they came back. My claws couldn't dig into the metal or glass of the truck. I had to rely on the traction of my paws to get me there.

When I reached the sled, I was able to wiggle my way into the sled bag, which had been left partially open. It was very full, loaded with stuff I'd never seen before. I pushed my way through to get to the sleeping bag that was always in the sled. I curled up on top and decided to take a long nap and wait for the adventure to start.

I woke to the crazed, chaotic sounds of dogs barking and yapping as they were getting loaded into the boxes on the truck. Once all the dogs were loaded, the truck roared to life. We headed out on our next quest. The constant hum of the engine and gentle rolling of the truck lulled me back to sleep.

I must have slept a long time, and when I woke the truck was no longer moving. I couldn't hear the dogs or Honey and Yes Dear. It was dark in the sled bag, and I wasn't able to tell if it was day or night. I was getting hungry, but I was trapped in the sled bag. I could smell salmon. Now if I could just wiggle my way past all this gear: snowshoes, ax, dog food bowls, bags of clothes, and a small cooler. There it was… a bag of salmon! It was sealed shut, but I was able to chew my way through the bag. That night I had a nice dinner of frozen salmon snacks. With nothing else to do and being alone in this dark sled bag, I decided to take another nap.

When I woke next, the sled was being moved off the truck. I heard Honey and Yes Dear talking outside the sled. They slid it backwards and tilted it steeply. I was lucky there was so much gear inside, or I would have slid to the back end of the sled. It hit the ground hard, but thankfully I was cushioned by the sleeping bag. It wasn't too long before I heard the dogs. They were calm at first, but soon they started getting excited. They must be getting ready to go for a run. I can't wait to poke my head out and surprise Honey. I wonder where we'll be.

The dogs were barking louder and louder. Then I noticed a lot of other dogs barking too. It sounded like all the dogs in the world were barking! The sled started lunging forward and backward as the dogs were pulling against it. I figured it must have been tied down. Finally, we started moving, but slowly, not the usual rocketing out of the dog yard. Honey kept calling to the dogs, "Easy guys, easy."

I don't think they wanted to go slow. Then I heard other voices all around. A loud, deep, muffled and somewhat staticky voice called, "30 seconds to go!"

"Have a great run Honey. I'm going to miss you!"

"Yes Dear, it should be fun. I'll miss you too!"

"10 seconds," the staticky voice called over the clamor of the dogs.

"Be safe," Yes Dear added.

92

"5, 4, 3, 2, 1, GO! And they're off, on their way to Nome!" The muffled voice continued.

Suddenly the sled launched forward with more force than I had felt before. We were on our way to Nome, wherever that is. Judging from all the added excitement outside the sled, I knew this was going to be one big adventure.

I stayed in the sled for a little while then decided I would surprise Honey and poked my head out.

"MICKEY! What are you doing? You can't be here! We're running the Iditarod. We'll be gone for too long. It's going to get too cold for you. You're likely to freeze to death."

He always worried too much about me. Dog sledding isn't that hard. I've been fine on all our other runs. This one won't be any different. I thought as I smiled back at him.

"Mickey, I can't believe you hid in the sled! How did you even get in there? I'll leave you at the first checkpoint, and they'll send you home."

"I'm not going home. I'm staying with you and my dogs," I glared at him. We settled into a long day's run. The brilliant sun skirted the tops of the trees as the day pressed on. We steadily and smoothly continued down the trail.

This trail was different than all the others I'd been on. It was flat and wide, and for much of the run, the trail was lined with people. Most of the time when we'd go on a run, we wouldn't see any other people. It was surprising to have so many watching us go by. As we passed, the people would cheer and wave. Little kids ran up close but stayed out of the dogs' way. As we passed them, Honey would hand old dog booties to them. They laughed in excitement and ran back to the others.

The dogs ran right by all the people without even a passing glance. They didn't care about the attention or cheers. The dogs just wanted to run and were too focused on the trail.

We ran most of the day then pulled the sled into a checkpoint. The checkpoint was chaotic with dogs and people all over the place. Some dogs were jumping and barking anxious to get running again. Others were calmly resting on cozy beds of straw.

People were scurrying around, some caring for the dogs, others hauling straw or gear bags around. I surveyed the other dog teams, my dogs looked better than all the others. As we pulled in, a man with a big puffy jacked and a face even hairier than Honey's hurried over to us. "Is that a cat on your sled? That's just crazy!" He exclaimed.

"I know. He hid in my sled. I didn't find him until we were already on the trail. I'd like to leave him here and have him sent home. Can I do that?"

"Of course you can. Crazy cat!" the man replied.

"Oh, you have no idea how crazy." Honey chuckled.

"What's that supposed to mean?" I looked at Honey questionably. "And NO WAY am I going home! This is my adventure also. I'm going to Nome with you and my dogs! Wherever that is."

Honey seemed to ignore my protests as he pulled some food out of the sled. "Mickey, let me get the dogs something to eat, and then I'll find someone to take care of you." He grabbed the bowls from the sled bag and placed one in front of each dog. Then he scooped a big heaping ladle full of thick meaty soup into each bowl. The dogs lapped their soup as Honey picked me up and carried me inside a building.

There were a lot of people inside but no dogs. It was noisy from the clamoring of so many voices talking. There was a fire blazing in the woodstove in the corner. The room was brightly lit and steamy hot from the crowds of people and fire. As we worked our way through the room, most people stopped what they were doing to stare and ask what I was doing there.

Honey tried to explain and asked if anyone could send me home. A young lady with long golden hair flowing out from under her colorful hat approached and stated that she was the head volunteer at this checkpoint. She assured Honey she could make sure I made it safely back home.

"Mickey, you crazy boy. You be good. I'll see you when I get home," Honey sadly whispered to me as he kissed me on the head and placed me in the arms of the lady. "Take care of him please. He's a great cat," Honey told her as his voice softly cracked.

There's no way I'm letting this lady send me home. I just started this adventure, and I'm going to finish it! All I needed now was an escape plan. The blonde lady sat down with me on her lap. She started petting me, softly stroking my head. "Well, this isn't so bad either," I thought. After all... it was toasty warm in this building, and I could smell meat cooking. Maybe she'd give me some hot food to eat.

I sat on her lap as Honey headed out the door. Before the door shut, he turned and cast a sad look my way. Tears were building in his eyes. Shortly after the door shut, I heard MY dogs barking. I know their bark. I can tell their bark from the other dogs' barks. I can also tell if they are barking because Honey is coming around with food or when there is a moose nearby. This was their bark before a run. That meant they were getting ready to leave! And here I was in this warm building sitting on a nice lady's lap all comfy and cozy.

Someone opened the door, and I could see Honey getting on the sled. Without thinking, I launched off the lady's lap and sprinted for the door while it was still open. I barely squeezed through before it slammed behind me. I dashed across the snow towards the sled, passing other dogs. Some were eating, others resting. When the dogs saw me they went crazy barking and jumping. I flashed right past them. They were helpless to do anything about it but bark.

I reached Honey just as he pulled the hooks out of the snow. The sled lurched forward. I sprang into the air and aimed for the sled, landing right on top in my usual spot. I sat up proudly like nothing was wrong, and they hadn't tried to leave without me. I shot a quick glance back at Honey.

"MICKEY! What are you doing? You can't come with us!" He hollered. "Whoa! Whoa!" he called to the dogs as he stepped on the brake. The trail was hard packed and icy. The brake did not dig in. The spikes of the brake screeched as they scraped along the ice. I'd heard that sound before. The dogs did not slow down. "WHOA Gizmo! WHOA Griffin! Whoa dogs! WHOA!" Honey cried louder.

"Don't stop guys! Keep going, or he'll leave me behind!" I called to them.

Copper, the oldest and biggest dog in the team turned his head back and gave me a look as if to say, "Glad you're still with us." He and the rest of my team ignored Honey and sped down the trail.

They didn't slow down until the lights of the checkpoint faded far behind us. They wanted to continue this adventure with me I think.

"Alright you crazy cat! I guess you're coming with us... at least until the next checkpoint," Honey grumbled.

We continued the rest of the day and into the night. Mostly we followed a frozen river and wound through beautiful wilderness. The ice on the river was flat and smooth, but there was plenty of snow on it for grip. The river was wide and lined by towering trees coated with fluffy snow. We didn't see any wildlife. However, there were a lot of other dog teams with us on the river. Some of the teams passed us, and others we passed. Teams even rested on the side of the trail. As we passed one team resting, the dogs were enjoying a snack. The person gave us a funny look and hollered, "Is that a CAT?"

"No, it's a hood ornament!" Honey replied sarcastically. "A cat? That's crazy, who would bring a cat on Iditarod?"

The guy gave us an even funnier look as we continued on. I didn't leave my spot on the sled all day, but as it started to get late, I got tired and cold. I decided to crawl into the sled and get some rest.

I don't know how long I slept, but when I woke up, we were not moving. Everything was quiet. I peeked out of the sled, and the dogs were all curled up on straw sleeping soundly. Honey was in his sleeping bag next to the sled. They were all tired and sleeping, but I'd just had a long nap.

I hopped out of the sled and decided to take a walk around and explore for a little while. I did not get very far before I realized that was a bad idea. Every way I turned there was another team of dogs. Most were either sleeping or eating. These weren't my dogs. I did not know how they would react to me, and I did not want to find out either.

It was pretty cold, so I decided I could use a little more sleep. I snuck up to Copper who was sound asleep on a nice bed of straw and wiggled my way into his warm soft belly. Toasty warm, I curled up for a little more sleep. After I snuggled in, Copper gave me a soft lick on the top of my head and curled his tail up over the top of me. Then we both settled in for a good night's sleep.

12

The Iditarod, Still

"Mickey, Mickey, where are you?" Honey was frantically searching the sled for me. He stood up and looked all around the sled. Then staring down the trail and into the woods, he continued to shout, "Mickey, Mickey!"

Copper let out a soft short bark. Honey turned, and Copper lifted his tail showing him I was safe and warm. He came over and knelt next to us. He leaned over and kissed Copper on the head as he rubbed his face. "Good boy, Copper. Good boy! Thank you for watching over Mickey."

The early morning sun was just starting to cast beams of light through the tops of the trees. The summits of the mountains that surrounded us glowed with a brilliant red hue. There were no clouds in the sky. The air was cold, but not bitterly. This checkpoint was bustling with other dog teams, some still sleeping but most getting ready for another day's run. All around us, dogs were lapping up their breakfast or getting booties put on by their musher. A few were already harnessed and jumping and barking anxiously to get back out on the trail.

"Who's hungry? Let's get you all some food and then get on the trail. What do you say?" Honey exclaimed excitedly as he spooned out large portions of a meat soup for the dogs and a much smaller portion for me. I get fed well at home, but trail food is so hardy and meaty that I'm going to be spoiled. After the dogs finished eating, Honey knelt next to each dog, hugged them, and held them while talking softly too them. Even with my great hearing I couldn't make out what he said to each of them.

As he knelt, he gently held each paw in his hand and slipped on little booties then pulled the strap tight to hold them on. I'm so glad he did not put any on me. I hate those things! Honey loaded the sled back up and placed me on top. "OK Mickey, looks like you're with us a bit longer!"

He then reattached all the lines between the dogs and the sled. Now our dogs joined the chorus of barking, as they got excited to get moving again. After he attached the last line, Honey stopped briefly in front of the leaders.

"You guys ready to get moving again?" He asked. The dogs responded with a combination of barks, howls, and jumps. Honey jogged to the back of the sled and hopped on the runners. He pulled the snow hooks. And off we went again, back out into the great Alaskan wilderness.

It was a long day on the trail, but a beautiful day. We did not see many other dog teams. After a few hours on the trail, Honey called to the leaders to go "gee.' The dogs diverted down a side trail that led to a small area of packed snow and small patches of straw. "Looks like another team stopped to rest here. Why don't we do the same guys? Whoa," Honey called as he slowly placed pressure on the brake to bring the team to an easy stop.

While we rested and enjoyed our snack, another team went down the trail past us. The driver waved as she went by but did not stop. She was bundled up in a big fluffy parka with the hood pulled over her head. I couldn't see her face, but her dogs were beautiful. They all looked very similar, bigger than most sled dogs with black and white long thick fur coats. They were all focused on the trail ahead of them, and none of them even turned to check out our team.

I liked this new adventure and wanted to see all I could, but at times I would get too cold or tired. I had to escape the freezing temperatures by crawling into the sled and taking a nap in the sleeping bag, which Honey always left open for me.

Most of the day was quiet, full of beautiful dogsledding. We stopped at another checkpoint but did not stay. Occasionally, we'd stop for a snack and a little rest once in a while, but most of the time we ran.

The trail was smooth, and there was a lot of snow. Honey commented to me a couple of times about how nice the trail was and how much snow we had. He kept saying that the snow would make the steps much easier. I'm not sure how the snow would make the steps easier. The steps at home are pretty easy without any snow.

"I think this is it Mickey, The Happy River Steps." There was a little uneasiness in Honey's voice. We were traveling on a trail that had so much snow. There were snow walls taller than the sled on our gee and haw. Most of the time I could only see dogs and snow.

"Hold on tight Mickey. This could be rough!" Honey exclaimed. All of a sudden, the lead dogs disappeared down a steep drop. Each pair of dogs quickly followed. This should be fun. The sled reached the edge and dropped. It was so steep I thought the sled would flip over, and Honey would end up in front of me.

The dogs knew we could go fast down the steep hill. Quickly, we picked up speed. I sank my claws deep into the sled bag to hold on tight. The hill was not that long, but right after it leveled off, the dogs dropped down another steep hill. Immediately they turned sharply, as the trail bent to the right. The sled slid to the edge of the trail and bounced off the wall of snow. The force of the sled hitting the wall jarred some snow loose causing a mini avalanched that dusted the sled. Honey and I were covered in a thin coating of soft snow. Because of the deep snow on the trail, Honey was able to slow the dogs down a little.

As we rounded the turn, we dropped down the third cliff on a hill then leveled off onto a frozen river with a nice thick layer of snow. Honey was right; the steps were easy. At the bottom, there was a person just off the side of the trail bundled up in a thick heavy coat. He was half covered in snow taking pictures as we went by. I wondered where that person had come from since he didn't have any dogs with him.

The person took a few pictures as we went by. Then he quickly looked away from his camera and up at us. "Is that a CAT?" he yelled.

"No, just a real small sled dog. A cat? That's crazy, who would bring a cat on Iditarod?" Honey yelled back.

"How dare he call me a sled dog? I'm a cat! In fact, I'm Mickey the Mushing Cat!" I hollered back.

Soon after the three steep hills, we crossed a frozen river and headed up one long steep hill. Honey ran behind the sled pushing as we slowly made our way up the hill. "Come on Mickey, get off and push."

"Yeah right, me push? That's your job."

We pulled into another checkpoint. Honey got the dogs settled in, fed and bedded down for a rest. "Let's take a bit of a rest guys, OK? The steps were not bad today, but I don't want to do the gorge in the dark. We'll get some food and sleep, then head back out in the morning."

The gorge didn't sound good, I thought. It sounds kind of scary. Maybe I should have gone home? What was I thinking? This is the most fun I've ever had!

After Honey finished taking care of the dogs, he picked me up, rubbed his furry face on my head and tucked me in his jacket. "Let's go inside and get something to eat, Mickey. I think they might have something good inside for you. Let's go see."

There were a lot of dogs lined up outside, mostly sleeping. I didn't think they could see me inside his jacket. Maybe that's why he put me there and did not let me walk inside. The snow at the checkpoint was hard packed and squeaked with each step as we approached a small log cabin.

Smoke poured out of the brick chimney that rose above the snow-covered roof. The door creaked as we entered. Honey was careful to close it gently so it didn't slam shut. Inside was packed with people. Most were sitting around eating, but a few were lying on the floor at one end of the room sleeping. The air was thick, hot, and moist. Worse, it reeked of people that desperately needed a shower. Yet, that smell was overpowered by the luscious aroma of meat sizzling on a grill. Honey walked up to a counter, "Can I get two cheeseburgers, one without the bun, a cup of coffee and a glass of milk please?" Honey asked a tall dark haired older looking lady.

"Sure thing." She smiled and gestured towards a table "Have a seat. I'll bring it to you."

"Thanks." Honey smiled back. Then he turned, his bulky snow boots thumped on the wood floor as he lumbered to a nearby table and plopped down in a chair. He unzipped his jacket, and I settled down onto his lap. "Hey Kristy, how's your run going?" Honey called out.

Oh, our friend, Kristy, from back home was here? I didn't know she'd be out here with us. Her big smile and cheerful personality always brightened up the room. Her long blond hair, as always, was twisted around itself like two tails down each side of her face flowing out from under her bright purple hat.

"Mickey? What's he doing here with you?" She half screamed, half chuckled as she saw me sitting quietly waiting for my food.

"Somehow he hid in my sled. I didn't find him until I was halfway to Yentna. He wouldn't stay behind so he's coming with me for as long as he can take it. I think he'll want to stay inside once it starts getting really cold."

Our food arrived, and Honey broke up one burger and poured the milk on a plate for me. He ate his food and talked with Kristy while I ate. Kristy praised her dogs, saying how wonderful they were doing so far. No matter how tired or cold, she was always excited and enthusiastic about her dogs and mushing. Honey seemed tired but he perked up quite a bit listening to her talk about her run.

"I'm having a great run also. All that snow on the steps made it fun, not at all scary. I guess I got lucky this year," Honey mumbled with a mouth half full of burger.

"How long are you staying?" Kristy asked.

"I want to do the gorge in the daylight, so I plan to leave first light," Honey replied.

"I'll follow you out in case you have trouble. The gorge is one of the toughest parts of the trail, but also one of my favorites. It's a lot of fun."

I guess she'd been out here before. It was good to see our friend, but I wanted to get outside and curl up with Copper again now that I had a full belly. The two of them chatted while finishing their meals. Finally, they both declared they were exhausted and needed some rest. We all headed back out to our teams for the night where I curled up against Copper's warm belly again. Honey slept in his sleeping bag next to the team.

Honey woke us all up while it was still dark. He fed the dogs and then me. He sat and ate with me next to the sled while the dogs ate. Then Honey loaded the sled back up, gave me a hug and put me on top. Off we went to the gorge, whatever that had in store for us.

The trail started nice and slow. I wondered what all the concern was about. As the sun started getting higher in the sky, the trail started heading downhill. It did not start very steep, but it slowly got steeper and steeper. After what seemed like hours, I wondered if this hill would ever end.

The trail was long and narrow, and there was a tall wall of rock on one side of us. The rock wall went up for as far as I could see, casting a dark shadow across the trail. Jagged fangs of ice clung to the rock wall as if a frozen dragon was waiting to engulf any team that took too long to get through this gorge. A haze of frozen mist shrouded the eyes of the dragon and obscured the top of the wall.

On the other side of the trail was a partially frozen river. There were holes in the river ice, and I saw the water below was moving fast. It churned over rocks and under ice ledges that jutted out above the river. Many of the rocks in the river were being washed downstream by the swift current. The rocks that stood tall above the flow were crusted in crystal ice and sparkled in the morning light.

I'd hate to fall off the sled now and end up in that water. The dogs were moving fast, and we zigzagged back and forth over the river on narrow bridges of ice. On both sides of the ice bridges was the fast-flowing open river. I was holding on as hard as I could but thought it might be best to hide inside the sled. I stood up and turned around to get to the opening in the sled bag. Right then, we took a sharp turn across an ice bridge. I saw the cold water flowing right under us. I wasn't sure there was enough ice on the bridge for the sled. The sled slid to the edge of the bridge, and one of the runners was off the bridge and over the open water. Honey had a terrified look on his face.

"Mickey get inside the sled now!" He shouted.

I was trying to get in the sled but stopped, mesmerized and terrified by the river below. Just then we took another sharp turn to the right. We'd just crossed the ice bridge, and the trail was slick. The sled did not follow the dogs around the tight turn but slammed into the side of the rock wall really hard. The hard hit into the wall threw me off the sled. I landed, feet first of course, in a thin layer of snow between the trail and the river.

"Whoa, Whoa!" Honey called to the dogs, but they did not stop. The trail was too icy for the sled break to dig in and stop the sled. Honey turned and looked at me "MICKEY! I'll come get you as soon as I can stop them! Whoaaaaaaa! WHOAAA!" he hollered as the sled continued down the trail.

I stood in the snow watching them disappear around another bend in the trail. I was alone, all alone. I didn't know where I was and hadn't felt this alone since before I had been rescued. An empty hollow feeling I hadn't felt in years descended on me in an instant. I didn't know if the team would be able to stop and come back to get me.

I decided I should start walking to try and catch up with them. I only walked for a few minutes before a team of dogs flew by me, two at a time. "On by, on by!" I heard a loud but calm voice call out as the dogs listen and ran on by.

"Hey, was that Jonah in lead of that team," I wondered to myself. "I know that dog."

As the team passed, a hand grabbed me around my belly and picked me up and pulled me in close. "KRISTY! It was Kristy. She'd got me!" I was so relieved. I calmed down a little and tried to figure out how she'd done that. She'd steered the dogs around those tough turns, over the ice bridge and with one hand picked me up.

She stuffed me inside her jacket, my head sticking out facing her. I rubbed my head on her face to thank her for saving me. She kept me in her jacket until we came up to Honey and my dogs.

"Kristy did you see Mickey out there?" Honey yelled in a very anxious voice, "he fell off the sled, and I couldn't stop the team."

"Don't worry. I got him. Here he is," she said removing me from her warm coat and handing me over to Honey.

"OH, THANK YOU! I knew this was a bad idea, letting him stay with me. I think I need to send him home at the next checkpoint."

"I don't know. He seems fine. I think he's having fun." Kristy said.

That was a bit too scary for me, but I am having fun. I'm not ready to go home yet. I want to finish this adventure.

Honey grabbed me, hugged and thanked Kristy again a few more times. Then he zipped me up inside his jacket. "Are you cold? Want to stay in my jacket for a little while?" he asked. It was nice and warm in there, but I could not see where we were going. I think HE needed me to be close for a little while, so I decided to let him keep me in his jacket for the rest of the day.

We continued on the trail, stopping from time to time at different checkpoints. At some we stayed, ate, and slept. Others we just went straight through and back on the trail. We had a few areas of rough trail, but not as rough as we'd been through already.

The days continued one after another. It was starting to seem like the trip in the RV, which I thought would never end. Eventually the RV trip ended. I'm sure once this adventure is over, we'll go home and see Yes Dear and my friend, Beans, again.

13

We Made It!

We stopped at many more checkpoints. People started calling me by name and saying hi. They often stopped by while we were taking care of the dogs or eating. They wanted to pet me and talk to Honey for a little while.

"Mickey is becoming famous. Everyone from Willow to Nome knows about him by now," one person explained to Honey.

"He's a great cat. The dogs love him, and he's having a fantastic time. He's spent the past few winters on the sled training with me. Mickey might as well go to Nome with me," Honey replied.

The best part of becoming popular was that everyone wanted to feed me. One brutally cold morning we were resting in a small town along a wide frozen river. The sun was up, but it was not quite light out. The clouds were thick and obscured the sun's glow. Light crystalline flakes whipped sideways as a stiff wind blew across the river ice and through town.

"The Yukon River is known for the windstorms Mickey. We are just in Anvik. We'll be on the river and in this weather for a while. Try to stay out of the wind, and it won't be as bad," Honey explained to me as he fed the dogs.

I huddled on the downwind side of the sled. Out of the wind, it wasn't too cold. In the wind it was unbearable for me. The dogs don't seem to mind the wind though. They had all gotten used to the routine and stood quietly waiting for their meal. Somehow they were able to ignore the gale blowing in their faces.

The dogs always got fed first, and I didn't mind waiting since the dogs were doing most of the work on this trip. While I waited for my breakfast, a young girl with hair as black as my fur strolled up towards us. She stopped a few feet away and stood quietly. She was wearing a long coat made from animal fur I'd not seen before. Her hair was tucked down the back of her coat and the hood was pulled over her head. The hood was lined with a lush silvery white fur rim.

She looked warm bundled up in that coat as she waited patiently until Honey was done feeding the dogs and me. After we were done, she softly spoke to Honey, "Hi, my name is Amka. May I give Mickey a present?

"Of course you can. Thank you so much," Honey said joyfully ending with a big smile.

She handed him a blanket, "I made it for him when I heard that he was out on the trail with you. It's a blanket, but you can wrap it around him and use it like a jacket. I knitted it from the fur of my dogs. I hope he likes it. I hope it keeps him warm too. It's supposed to get very cold out there the next couple of days."

"He's going to love this!" Honey exclaimed as he wrapped the soft, black, white and grey furry blanket around me. It covered my body and had a little hole for me to tuck my head into to keep it from falling off. It was soft and instantly blocked the wind from cutting through my fur.

If this was made from dog fur, I now knew why the wind didn't bother the dogs. There was still a strong scent of dog remaining in the fur, but it reminded me of my friend, Beans. I got a warm and sad feeling thinking of Beans and how I missed him. This new blanket would surely keep me warm for the rest of the trip. I tucked my head through the hole in the blanket so it wouldn't fall off and brushed past Honey to rub up against Amka's leg to thank her. She responded by crouching next to me and rubbing my head. "Have a good run Mickey. Stay safe," she said before standing up and turning to walk back towards the center of town.

I watched her until she slowly faded out of my view. What a wonderful, kind, young girl to have made such an effort to create a beautiful present for me. Her kindness warmed me as much as the blanket. Amka was right too, the next couple of days got bitterly cold. I spent most of the time in the sled on Honey's sleeping bag, wrapped in my new blanket, and I was still cold.

Once I poked my head out to see what was happening. All the dogs were wearing their jackets now. They only wore them when it was very cold outside. I turned and looked at Honey. He had his biggest jacket on. His face was white with ice frozen to the hair on his face. He had icicles dangling from his nose, and one eye had ice crusting his eyelashes. It looked frozen shut. I was worried about him.

"Mickey, are you OK? It's pretty cold out here. You should stay in the sled," He said. "My thermometer reads 20 below. It's going to get even colder when the sun goes down. We better find a place to spend the night and try to stay warm." We found a spot just off the trail that was sheltered a little by some trees.

It was getting dark, and the temperature dropped with the sun. I waited in the sled while Honey fed the dogs. He'd brought some straw with us from the last checkpoint and laid it down for each dog. He adjusted their jackets to make sure they were secure and wouldn't fall off during the night. The dogs all curled up and quickly went to sleep after eating. I know the dogs don't mind the cold as much as I do. They seem to get more excited the colder it got.

"Mickey, look at the sky. It's so clear. Have you ever seen so many stars? It's beautiful." He whispered as he held me in his jacket. Together we gazed at the stars. While we were standing there, brilliant blue and green lights started flashing across the sky.

"Look Mickey! The Aurora, The Northern Lights!"

It was fantastic! Blue and green bands of light danced across the clear starry night sky. It was so wonderful even the dogs took time to look up and enjoy the sight. I could have watched all night except for the cold.

"It's getting colder Mickey. My thermometer only goes down to 40 below, and it hit bottom. I'm very worried I won't be able to keep you warm all night. What am I going to do with you?"

He unloaded all the gear from the sled then laid out some straw next to the sled. He placed his sleeping bag on the straw and then went and unhooked Copper from the line. He walked Copper over to the sled and placed him inside the sled. Copper lay there quietly, looking a little confused. Honey then went and brought Gracie and laid her in the sled next to Copper. He then put me in between the two dogs. Copper and Gracie lay close to each other, and I snuggled between them as they both curled their tails over top of me.

"You'll be warmer in there with them than you would be with me. They'll take care of you, Mickey. Won't you Copper and Gracie? I'll sleep out here in my bag. The straw will help keep me off the snow, and I should be warm enough. Maybe I'll put Daisy in the sleeping bag with me." He zipped the sled bag closed blocking out the stars and northern lights. It did help seal in the heat from Copper and Gracie. Snuggled between the two of them warmed me more than a brilliant summer sun could. I curled up tightly between them and stayed warm and cozy all night. I hoped Daisy would keep Honey just as warm. I slept soundly through the night until Honey unzipped the sled bag in the morning.

"Are you guys all warm and toasty in there? I wish there was room in there for me, but little Daisy kept me warm. It's another glorious morning. It should be another great day for a run. It's still

118

cold, but not as bad as it was last night. We should get moving."

I was so comfortable and toasty warm snuggled between my two furry furnaces that I didn't want to think about the frigid air outside. But both Copper and Gracie seemed anxious to get back on the trail and stood quickly. They looked around then hopped out of the sled. Honey gave them both big hugs and kisses and thanked them for taking care of me.

He started a fire in his cook pot. As the water in the pot started to boil, steam rose and filled the crisp morning air with the deep aromatic scent of cooking meat. Without Copper and Gracie to keep me warm, I quickly felt the cut of bitter air. The hot bowl of soup warmed me from the inside and gave me the energy and strength to get my day started. Once we were all done eating, we got back on the trail. It was still bitterly cold, and although I hated to miss the beauty of the land we traveled through, I spent most of the day in the sled bag trying to stay warm.

The next couple of days remained brutally cold. I don't think I would have survived without Amka's blanket. Even with the added warmth of the blanket, Honey had one of the dogs curl up with me in the sled to help keep me warm at night. We spent the coldest nights at checkpoints. That way Honey and I could sleep inside where it was warm.

I think he wanted to spend more time on the trail but was worried about me.

We made it to one checkpoint just as it was getting dark. Because of the darkness, I didn't get a good look around. We spent the night inside, and when we went outside in the morning everything looked different.

For days we'd been traveling on wide open snow or ice covered rivers through forests of towering spruce trees laced with sparkling ice crystals and laden with heavy snow. We'd also run through high mountain passes flanked by towering rugged peaks and descended through steep narrow gorges, but now it was all different. Here there was a beach, like the beach back home where we'd go clamming. Only this beach was covered in snow and ice.

There were no waves softly lapping on the wet send. This water was completely frozen, like the rivers. At home I could see mountains in the distance over the water, but no mountains towered in the distance here. There was only ice as far as I could see. Nothing else was out there, just ice.

"Look Mickey, it's Norton Sound. We made it to the coast. We're almost to Nome. We've got to be careful today. If we make a wrong turn out there, we'll end up crossing the Bering Sea and wind up in Siberia. That's if there is no open water. Let's hope

Gizmo and Griffin follow the trail across the sound to Nome."

The dogs and I got a warm steamy bowl of thick meat soup. After eating I took a short nap in the sled while Honey filled his belly with a warm meal also. Like after every meal, we let the dogs rest a bit before we headed back out on the trail.

I sat on top of the sled and surveyed our surroundings while Honey hooked up the dogs for the day's run. The sun's hazy light struggled to make its way through the thick layer of clouds overhead. Gazing out over the frozen sea, everything looked the same. It was all grey.

The sea ice seemed to merge with the sky. I couldn't tell where one ended and the other began. If we lost sight of land, we could get lost out there very easily. It looked intimidating. For the first time since the gorge, I felt hesitant about today's run.

Yet, this was part of our adventure. We would never know what was out there if we didn't go. The trail ahead looked daunting. Somehow I knew I'd want to be outside to see everything today. My new blanket-coat was lying neatly on top of the sled. I slipped my head under one end and up through the hole so it lay over my back and hung around my neck.

"You guys ready?" Honey called calmly but firmly to the dogs. "How 'bout you Mickey?"

I nodded.

"Alright guys, let's go." The sled slid easily and silently out of town towards the frozen sea. Soon after, the trail climbed some small dunes then dropped onto the beach. Finally we ran out on the ice. The dogs followed what looked like scratches in the ice and posts that looked as if they were marking a trail. But, there was no real trail like we had been on before.

It did not take very long out on the sea trail before we couldn't see the checkpoint behind us. We could only see ice behind us and ice in front of us. In fact, we saw ice on all sides. Everything looked the same. The ice blended into the sky.

I could not tell where the ice ended and where the sky began. I sure hoped the dogs could figure out how to get across this ice to the next checkpoint. The day seemed to go on forever. There was nothing around to give us an idea of how fast we were going or how long we were out there. As long as we kept seeing the posts in the ice, I knew we were going the right way. I am sure the dogs knew that also.

Suddenly, the dogs stopped, right in the middle of nowhere. We could not see anything but ice. Why would they stop out here? "Gizmo, Griffin, what's the matter?" Honey asked. They just stood there, not moving. "Come on guys. Let's get going," he called. They still did not move. They stood motionless, almost frozen. Honey tried to set a hook in the ice, but the hook would not dig in. I knew he didn't want to get off the sled if he could not set his hook.

If the hook wasn't set, the dogs could take off without him. The dogs didn't seem to want to go anywhere, so Honey finally decided to walk up and see what was wrong with Gizmo and Griffin. He carefully slid his way up to them, softly petting each dog on the head as he passed.

"What's up guys? We shouldn't have that much further to go before we get to the next checkpoint." He tried to lead them ahead, but they would not move. He stood in front of them looking around.

"You know what guys, I don't see any trail markers out here. How did we get out here? Oh there they are, over that way. We're not far off the trail. Come on guys, follow me." The trail markers were off to our right a little. With the markers being far apart and no real trail, the dogs had accidentally drifted over to the left. Luckily for us, the trail was in sight.

"Come on Gizmo. Come on Griffin, this way," Honey encouraged, but they still didn't move. They refused to follow him towards the trail.

"OK guys, I'm going that way to the trail. You stay here if you want," Honey said, but he wasn't fooling me at all. I knew he would not leave us. He was just trying to trick the dogs to follow him. He took a few steps ahead of them and turned towards the dogs. "You guys coming or not?"

I guess not, because they didn't move. Honey took a few more steps, and Griffin let out a loud bark. Honey turned around. As he did the ice below his feet let out a light but long rippling cracking sound. He looked down and stopped in his tracks. His eyes widened with fear. Honey stood motionless for a couple seconds. "OK guys, now I know what you know, thin ice. Good dogs! Stay there. I'll come back to you, slowly."

The next few minutes were terrifying. It was only a few minutes, but seemed like hours as I helplessly watched Honey try to get back to the sled. My whole body tightened, and I felt knots twist and gnaw in my belly. I remembered that every fall Honey and Yes Dear would discuss how to tell when the lakes and rivers had enough ice to hold the team.

The horrific thought of crashing through thin ice into the fridge water below was now a real possibility for the man who loved and took care of us. It was a sickening feeling watching him. I knew there was nothing the dogs or I could do to help. As we stood motionless, he slowly and easily lay down on his belly. Then he slithered across the ice. He would move a little and stop when he heard more cracking, then move again when the cracking stopped. The cracking continued on and off until he was just a few feet from the dogs.

He lay motionless waiting and listening. When there was just silence, he slowly stood up and led the dogs, turning us around the way we came. Once he got them completely turned around, he let the dogs lead again. He knew they would stop if we hit more thin ice. As we made our way back to the last trail post, the tension started to ease. "Haw, haw," Honey called. The team swung around the trail posts. This time headed directly towards the next one, avoiding the area of thin ice.

Once we passed the next trail marker Honey called "whoaaaa," and the dogs eased to a halt. He still couldn't set the snow hook but trusted the dogs not to leave without him. Honey stood on the runners for a couple seconds taking a long deep breath and exhaling with a loud extended huff.

I glanced back to see him raise one shaky hand to his mouth, his eyes wide, staring into the distance. The realization of what almost happened sank into him, then me. My legs started trembling. I felt like I would throw up my breakfast. After a short pause, Honey slowly made his way up to the leaders. He knelt between Gizmo and Griffin. Tears rolled down his cheek as he put one arm around each of them and kissed the top of their heads.

"Good boys! You saved our lives." He spent a few minutes hugging and kissing all the dogs until he regained his composure. When he got back to the sled, he picked me up. After he hugged me too, he tucked me in his coat. Then he pulled out some salmon treats from the sled for all of us.

The dogs devoured their salmon like they always did. I still had knots in my stomach and was trembling a little. For the first time in my life, I couldn't eat. I'd been in trouble before, but this was the first time I feared for the safety of my family.

It was amazing the dogs knew there was thin ice and had not crossed it. I've learned spending so much time with my dogs that they are smarter than Honey. I think they might even be smarter than me.

"Not hungry Mickey? I can't eat either. I'm still shaking." He kissed me softly on the top of my head. "Don't worry. We're safe now. The dogs made sure of that. Even though we know the dogs won't run across thin ice, I still want to get onto solid ground again soon. Let's get to the next checkpoint. You guys ready?" He asked the dogs as he stepped back on the sled runners. "Let's go!" Honey called to the dogs.

As we were heading toward the checkpoint, I started wondering if it was time for me to go home. That had been a dangerous situation. Then I realized, once again the dogs made sure I was safe. They wouldn't let anything happen to me as long as we were together. A few hours later, we pulled up onto another beach and off the ice. We slipped up a small hill and into the next checkpoint. I was so glad we were off that ice. We spent the night at the checkpoint. The next morning, we headed back out on the trail.

"Alright guys, let's go. Only a couple more days and we'll be in Nome." We spent another good day on the trail and another night at a checkpoint. As we got ready to head back out, Honey took a little extra time giving all the dogs an extra-long hug. Then he picked me up and walked to the leaders. "This is it guys. Today's the last day. Seventy more miles and we'll be in Nome. It'll be like just another day training," Honey said, but I had a feeling today was more important to him than another day of training.

It was a beautiful sunny day. The weather was nice enough for me to spend the day on the sled. I didn't want to miss anything on our last day.

It was a long day. The dogs seemed tired. I think they were ready to go home. Each day they got up and ran and ran and ran. I kept thinking they would want to stop and go home, but they never did. Instead, they acted as if they didn't want to be anywhere but on the trail running. I should have known that from all the running they did back home. No matter how much they ran, they always wanted to go run more. Crazy dogs!

We were traveling along a frozen beach, a few miles from Nome, when Honey stopped for a little while. He gave us all a snack and spent time with each dog, petting each one on the head. He picked me up, kissed me on the head, and carried me up to the leaders. Then Honey knelt in front of the team. His eyes were watery, and there was a slight quivering to his voice as he spoke to us. "I'm so proud of all of you. I'm honored to have been able to spend this time with all of you. I'm never going to forget this trip. Now, let's go home!"

"Home!" the dogs barked and I cheered.

We were on the trail for about another thirty minutes. Then the trail turned right off the beach and onto the main street in Nome. The street was lined with people cheering and waving to us.

"Way to go!"

"Congratulations, you made it!"

"Great job, Mickey!"

At the end of the line of people was a larger group of people standing around an arch made of trees. "That's the burled arch Mickey. We made it!" Honey exclaimed, as we pulled up to the finish line. I saw Yes Dear waiting there under the arch. She ran up and hugged Honey, giving him a kiss. "Congratulations Honey! It's great to see you! I missed all of you so much." She kissed him one more time then picked me up and held me tight.

"Oh Mickey, I missed you. I hope you had fun!"

I was having such an adventure that I didn't realize how much I missed her warmth and caring until she held me. I held her tight and rubbed my head under her chin. She kissed the top of my head then zipped up her coat around me to keep me warm and close.

Honey hugged Yes Dear and me together. "We did it, Mickey! YOU did it, Mickey! You finished the Iditarod!"

Honey hugged and kissed all the dogs while Yes Dear and I were barraged with people wanting to take my picture or interview Honey about the race.

The scene under the burled arch was chaotic. There were so many people yelling questions with flashing lights of cameras. It was confusing and overwhelming. After being out on the trail with just Honey and the dogs for so long, all this noise and attention was too much for me. I wanted to turn around and go back out on the trail to be alone with Honey and my dogs.

OK, maybe not. I wanted to go home with Yes Dear and snuggle up with Beans next to a warm fire.

After the chaos of the finish line settled down, all the commotion was worth it. My picture was on the front page of two newspapers! I was on the Nome Nugget and the Anchorage Daily News. The next day Angel called to congratulate us. She told us she'd seen us on the national news. Angel said Honey should write a book about our adventures.

14

Old Man Beans

Our wonderful but long adventure ended with a less exciting trip home. We had a long flight then a long drive in the truck. I knew we were finally home when I heard the ever-increasing roar of our dogs as they welcomed us home. The truck eased to a stop just in front of the dog yard.

The dogs drowned out the sound of the engine. I couldn't tell when Honey shut off the motor. As soon as he opened his door, I leaped off his lap and darted out the door. I hit the ice-covered ground, my rear legs skidding out from under me. I landed belly first on the cold hard ground. I dug my claws into the ice and scampered back to my feet then took off towards Beans.

All the dogs were running around and jumping except Beans. He stood tall and proud facing us and greeting us with a loud but rhythmic bark. I was so excited to see him that I ran right past Nikko. After my swipe across his nose, I've never been sure if he would retaliate. So, he was the one dog I usually kept my distance from. Nikko was too excited about the return of the rest of the pack to even notice me.

I approached Beans and tried to stop but my feet wouldn't slow down on the ice. I dug and clawed at the ice but slid right into Beans' large front legs. It knocked my legs out from under me. As I lay on the ice, Beans' massive wet dripping tongue dragged across my face. It was wet but warm and welcoming.

I regained my footing and slid in and out of his legs and under his belly rubbing my head on his thick fur. We sat together watching as Honey and Yes Dear returned the Iditarod team dogs to their homes. After all the dogs were settled in, they took a long time to greet the rest of the dogs. Then they fed and gave every dog a fresh bed of straw. I had a wonderful experience on the trail with my team, but it was comforting to be home with all my dogs again. I couldn't wait to sleep in our home again with both Honey and Yes Dear.

After that adventure, what else could we do that would be more exciting? I couldn't think of anything better than our time on the trail with Honey and the dogs. If only Beans was young enough to have joined us.

That winter came to an end, and we had another fun summer fishing, clamming and kayaking. The next winter was similar to the previous. Honey and Yes Dear went on many adventures. They would take me on some of the trips, but usually they would leave me home. The neighbor boy, Willy, would come over and take care of me. He also took care of any dogs that did not go on a trip. I missed Honey and Yes Dear when I didn't join them, but I didn't miss the cold. It was nice to have a warm home to sleep in at night. I also missed getting outside to see my friend Beans.

One time, when Willy was leaving, I snuck out the door without him noticing. I hid behind the woodpile until he left then ran to see Beans. I stopped by to say hi to Beans. Then I ran through the snow and hunted for a few mice. I was outside a while before it started getting dark. Then I realized I was getting cold. I went back to the front door to go inside, but nobody was home to let me in. Willy had gone for the night and would not be back until the next day.

The sun was sinking below the trees, and the light breeze was getting stronger. It cut through my fur, and I didn't have my blanket. Because I had been hunting in the snow for hours, my feet were wet and now ice was forming crystals on my toes.

My paws, nose and ears were stinging from the ice and wind. A hollow empty feeling crushed my spirits in an instant. It's been a long time since those days in the cold barn, and I haven't felt this lonely since then. I tried to calm myself by remembering that Honey and Yes Dear had taken great care of me. They'd done so much to make sure I wasn't alone. They had not abandoned me and would come home, but until then, I needed to find a way to stay warm. I started walking around looking for a place to endure what looked to be a long frigid night.

As I searched for a warm place to sleep, I heard a bark. BEANS! Beans was barking at me. No, Beans was barking for me. In an instant the fear and loneliness disappeared as I realized I was not alone. I had my friend Beans. I ran over to Beans. He gave me his usual big slobbery kiss and then nudged me into his house. It was surprisingly warm inside with a nice soft bed of straw. Beans followed me in and curled up around me, nearly suffocating me. But, he kept me warm and toasty all night.

The following morning I awoke to the sound of Willy coming to feed the dogs. As Beans woke up and started to get up for breakfast, I stopped him. I licked his face to let him know how much I appreciated him keeping me warm all night. He probably saved my life.

When Willy saw me, he ran to me calling, "Mickey? Mickey! What are you doing outside? Are you OK?"

"I am, thanks to Beans," I purred while rubbing my head on his leg.

When Honey and Yes Dear came home from their adventure, Willy told them that I had gotten out and spent the night with Beans. They were not upset with me for sneaking out. Instead, they hugged and kissed Beans in gratitude for taking care of me.

The next day we were all headed out for a day of dog sledding. Honey and Yes Dear harnessed the dogs and put them out on the line in front of the sled. Beans, who usually runs around barking until he gets his harness, did not get out of his house to join the commotion and quietly watched, as the rest of the dogs got ready for the run.

Honey walked over to Beans with his harness. "Beans, don't you want to go for a short run today?" Beans just looked up at Honey but did not move. Honey knelt down and patted Beans on the head. "OK, old man, you can stay home and rest." He stood back up and jogged towards the sled. "Looks like Beans is staying home today, so that's everyone. Are you ready Mickey? Let's go!"

I really wanted to go. It had been a week since I had the chance to be out on the trail dogsledding. The dogs were all barking and jumping ready to hit the trail. The excitement and volume increased with every moment we waited. The thrill and anticipation of getting back out with my dogs tugged and drew me to the sled.

As I trotted to the sled, I glanced back to see Beans all alone in his house. I stopped in my tracks. I knew that lonely empty feeling that I saw in his eyes. He was a proud sled dog and had spent his life living to run. Now age was catching up with him, and the long runs were too hard on his aging muscles and joints.

I was drawn back into that feeling of isolation when I was locked out of the house. Beans had been there to comfort me and keep me warm. Now he was at a time in his life where he must be feeling isolated. I couldn't desert my friend and leave him alone today. I turned and bound through the snow back to Beans. I climbed over his head and into his house and curled up with him.

"Well Honey, it looks like Mickey wants to stay with Beans."

"Yes Dear, they'll be fine together. Let's go."

They were gone most of the day while Beans and I slept. The afternoon sun shone bright and warmed the crisp winter air. We got up to enjoy the afternoon warmth, chased each other around, then basked in the sun's rays and dozed back off. We were woken up by the teams return home. As after every run, all the dogs got a salmon snack, even Beans and me.

"Honey, do you think it's time for Beans to retire and join us in the house?"

"Yes Dear, I think you're right. If he was too tired to go for a run after us being away for a week, I think he's ready to retire."

Honey gently took Beans by the collar and led him into the house. Yes Dear and I followed close behind. Beans was a little unsure of what to do at the door. He had spent his entire life outside with the rest of his team. I walked past him, brushing against his leg to encourage him into the house. I stopped and turned to let him know he should follow me.

He slowly poked his head through the doorway and glanced around. He stopped with just his front paws in the doorway, unwilling to continue. Beans was never unsure of anything in all the time I'd known him. He was a strong dominant leader able and willing to charge headfirst through brutal storms and unknown terrain. Yet, this major change in his life had him apprehensive. I confidently strutted over to Beans, raised my head up to his chin, and rubbed him briefly then went back inside, as if to say, "This is now OUR home Beans. Come on in."

Beans slowly followed me inside and down the hall to the woodstove. I think Honey and Yes Dear knew this day was coming, because Honey brought out a large blue mat. It was soft just like mine, only larger. He placed it in front of the woodstove and called to Beans. "Here Beans this is yours," Honey said as he lightly patted the mat.

Beans was used to sleeping on a bed of soft warm straw not a cushy mat. This was all new to him. I strolled by him brushing against his leg as I passed then laid down on his new mat. Beans seemed to understand. He slowly walked over and joined me. Honey and Yes Dear sat on the floor next to us slowly caressing our heads and backs. Together we all enjoyed the warm fire.

15

Beans and Me

It didn't take long for Beans to get used to sleeping inside the house. He loved the glowing warmth of the woodstove just as much as I did. We spent most of our time together. At night we would either curl up together by the woodstove or join Honey and Yes Dear on their bed.

During the day, we often went for short walks together and would always stop and say hi to the rest of the dogs. We liked romping through the deep snow that no one had packed down yet. Beans always lead the way. He'd charge his way through light fluffy snow sending clouds of white crystals into the air falling back on me as I followed close behind. I'd leap from one of his paw prints to the next to avoid the really deep snow.

On the bitterly cold days, the snow was light and fluffy and did not stick to my feet. It was easy to shake the snow off. When the sun warmed the snow, it would get soft and wet, sticking to my fur and soaking my paws.

One day Beans and I took an extra-long walk. It was getting late in the winter, and the days were starting to warm up. We made it out to the dogsledding trail. The trail was packed hard and was easier to walk on than the deep snow. The sun was warm and bright and soothing on my black fur.

The warm sun also melted a thin layer of the hard-packed trail making it slippery, but my claws and the ruff pads on Beans' paws gave us both good traction. I think Beans really missed being out on the trail with his team. He stopped suddenly and looked intensely down the trail. He might be old, but his hearing was still good, better than mine.

It took me a little longer, but then I heard it too. A dog team was heading our way down the trail. The soft jingling of the dog collars and the light whoosh of the sled runners on the snow was all the noise the team made. The light breeze through the tree branches made more noise than all those dogs heading our way. The team rounded a bend in the trail. We sat and watched the beauty and grace of the dogs, as they ran closer. As they got nearer, three dogs suddenly ran out from the trees, down the trail, straight for the team.

I remembered those dogs. They would often chase our team down the trail, barking and growling as they chased us. They'd kept enough distance from our dogs as not to risk getting bitten. One of these dogs was large with long golden fur and was big and stocky. He was the fastest of the three. The smaller dogs were both black and white. One was much smaller than the other with very short fur and a large blocky head. The third dog had some wisps of grey in his fur and seemed more hesitant about chasing us. Instead, he simply followed his companions in the chase.

Our team usually just ignored them and kept running. The only thing that will distract a sled dog from running is food. They would not even give these dogs a glance as we passed. As this dog team ran smoothly past, only a few dogs gave an annoying sneer at the other dogs. The three dogs had jumped off the trail back into the trees, out of the way. They barked and growl as the team passed then turn to give chase.

We sat with the warm sun on our backs. A light breeze washed the scent of spruce over us as we watched the beautiful team moving in unison down the trail. Seeing them, I remembered Honey telling Yes Dear many times how much he loved watching dogs run. He would say how beautiful a team of dogs was. You know, he was right. As the team passed, most of the dogs completely ignored us, though a few turned to look at us but continued running. Only one dog barked and pulled towards us.

"Chinook, on by," the person on the sled exclaimed. The dog listened and continued running right on by us. I know Chinook! He's one of our friend's, Jane's, lead dogs.

"Hi Beans! Hi Mickey! What are you two doing out here? Be careful! Those dogs are out again." She pointed back down the trail towards the three dogs chasing her team.

The big golden dog was leading the other two in an all-out sprint trying to catch Jane's team, but all three slid to a stop when they noticed us. They only hesitated for a split second then charged Beans and me. There were three of them and only two of us. I was a bit smaller than they were. I looked at Beans, then turned and sprinted back towards home.

I knew if we could make it to the dog yard, we'd be safe. Beans didn't follow me. He stood his ground. He turned slightly to watch me run, making sure I was getting away. The three dogs were gaining ground and getting closer to him. Beans' ears lay back. His fur stood up on his neck.

His tail rose up, but not wagging. He pulled his lips back baring his teeth and growled like a low rolling thunder.

Beans was such a gentle dog. I had never heard him growl before. I wouldn't be much help in a fight, but I was worried Beans was outnumbered and too old to defend himself against that pack alone. I couldn't leave my friend alone.

He had helped me too many times before. Now it was my turn to help him. Beans turned to see if I had made it to safety. When he saw that I was running back to help him, he turned and charged towards the oncoming dogs. I knew he wanted this fight to be over before I got close enough to get hurt.

Beans ran full speed and dove at the lead dog, clamping his jaws down on the dog's left shoulder. Beans twisted his head pulling out a chunk of golden fur and skin. The dog let out a high pitch shriek, spun around, and took off back the way he came. Then Beans lunged at the smaller black and white dog, again driving his teeth into his left shoulder.

This dog was smaller but more ferocious than the large golden dog. He let out a loud vicious growl and twisted to the left in an attempt to sink his teeth into Beans. Beans might be old, but he was still fast and twisted his head to the right escaping the jaws of the smaller dog. As Beans twisted his head, he lifted the other dog up then slammed him to the ground. Standing over the dog, he wrapped his jaws around the dog's throat. Yet, he didn't clamp down. Beans did not want to kill the dog, just let him know that he was the boss around here.

The third dog reached Beans and drove his teeth into Bean's rear end just as I got close enough to get into the fight. I let loose and dove onto the back of the greying dog who had his teeth in Beans. I sank my claws into his back as deep as I could while simultaneously chomping down hard on his right ear with my teeth.

The dog yelped and let go of Beans then shook hard tossing me into the deep snow on the side of the trail. As I hit the snow, he turned. The skin on his nose wrinkled up and his lips drew back showing his sharp teeth. He let out a long, low guttural growl. I sprung back to my feet knowing my only defense was my speed.

I stood with my hair standing up to make me look larger. My ears were back. I was terrified, but I would not run and leave Beans. I twitched anticipating the dog's next move. Beans didn't wait for the greying dog's next move. Instead he instantly spun around placing himself between the dog and me. Beans let out a slow rolling, deep growl. His nose was curled up, fangs dripping with blood from the other two dogs.

The greying older dog didn't want to take on Beans. He slowly put his tail between his legs. Then he turned quickly and scurried down the trail. Old Man Beans had just taken on three dogs and risked his life to protect me. There was no better way he could have proven we were friends. In fact, we would be for the rest of our lives.

Beans stood above me waiting for the other dogs to gain some distance between them and us. When they were far enough away, Beans leaned down and nudged me a little with his nose to see if I was hurt. I was fine, not hurt at all. The deep snow had cushioned my fall. Thankfully, I hadn't been bitten.

Beans had only been bitten in his rear end and had a little blood staining on his black and grey fur. We had enough excitement for the day and slowly strolled home. When we got back to the dog yard, all the dogs were running around barking. They were excited because they'd heard our fight. Beans strutted through the yard, head and tail held high. He was proud. He had been king of this kennel for a long time. Now he was king of the neighborhood! I walked alongside him with my head and tail as high as I could hold them. I was proud to be friends with Beans.

Honey greeted us at the door and let us inside. "Beans, is that blood on your back? How'd that happen? Let me see." He knelt next to Beans and wiped aside the matted fur taking a closer look. "Looks like you've been bitten. Who did that Beans? It better not have been one of our dogs. You'll be fine, but let's clean that up."

Honey washed the area well and made sure the bleeding had stopped before he sat next to Beans holding him and softly whispering in his ear words I could not hear. Then he stood up pointing to the woodstove. "The fire's going. Why don't you guys go warmed up and rest."

The day had not been cold, but the fire in the woodstove gave off a soothing heat. It warmed our bodies and souls. Beans, tired and probably a bit sore, lay down on his mat next to the woodstove. I nudged my way up to his belly and curled up with him. He curled his tail over top of me. Together, we slept the rest of the day away, just Beans and Me.

Mickey's Tale

<u>The Adventures of Mickey the Mushing Cat</u> is a fictional story. However, the idea was based off the real life of Mickey, a wonderful friend who really was rescued as a stray cat by four angels, lived in Vermont, and moved to Alaska where his owners ran a kennel for dog mushing.

If you are looking for a new pet, please consider adopting from your local animal rescue shelter. Who knows what adventures they may take you on!

Made in the USA
Middletown, DE
21 December 2020